I0062742

THE NATION OF INNOVATION

Why Americans are more innovative
than any other nation?

Comparative Analysis of
Entrepreneurial and Innovative Context:
US versus Europe

MEL ARAT

Copyright © 2023 by Mel Arat

All rights reserved. No part of this publication may be reproduced, distributed, or transmitted in any form or by any means, including photocopying, recording, or other electronic or mechanical methods, without the prior written permission of the publisher, except in the case of brief quotations embodied in critical reviews and certain other noncommercial uses permitted by copyright law. For permission requests, write to the publisher, addressed "Attention: Permissions Coordinator," at the address below.

New York City Books
www.nycitybooks.com

217 Peace Pipe Way
Georgetown TX 78628 USA

Printed in the United States of America

Publisher's Cataloging-in-Publication data
Arat, Mel
Nation of Innovation

I-ISBN: 978-1-0881-2616-5

LCCN: 2023908818

THE NATION OF INNOVATION

Why Americans are more innovative than any other nation?

*Comparative Analysis of
Entrepreneurial and Innovative Context:
US versus Europe*

MEL ARAT

New York City Books

"Mel Arat's 'Nation of Innovation' is a captivating journey through the heart of American ingenuity. With meticulous research and vivid storytelling, Arat unveils the unique tapestry of factors that have ignited innovation in the United States. This book is a tribute to the dreamers, inventors, and entrepreneurs who have shaped the world we live in today. A must-read for anyone seeking to understand the dynamic spirit that defines the American experience."
Hakan Turgut, Author of Financial IQ

"Mel Arat's 'Nation of Innovation' is a tour de force that brilliantly captures the essence of American exceptionalism. Arat explores the question that has intrigued minds for centuries: Why has America been a hotbed of innovation? This book delves into the economic, cultural, and social dynamics that have fostered an environment where ideas flourish. A compelling read that unveils the secrets behind America's innovation legacy."
Necdet Buyukbay, International Business Consultant

Imagination's Flight

In the land where dreams take flight,
A tapestry of innovation woven tight,
From sea to shining sea, a boundless quest,
American spirit, innovation's blessed guest.

Inventors' minds, like stars in the night,
Illuminate pathways with creative light,
From Wright's soaring plane to Tesla's spark,
American life is innovation's embark.

Edison's bulb, a beacon of glow,
Illuminating streets where dreams grow,
Telephones ring, connecting the miles,
Innovation's magic, spanning diverse styles.

In Silicon Valley's digital domain,
Bill Gates and Jobs, a technological reign,
Computers hum, a symphony of code,
American life, in innovation's abode.

CONTENTS

When you're born you get a ticket to the freak show. When you're born in America, you get a front row seat.
George Carlin

1. INTRODUCTION

The United States of America has garnered a renowned reputation as a nation of innovation, consistently at the forefront of groundbreaking inventions and pioneering industries. Visionary American inventors and entrepreneurs, such as the Wright Brothers, Thomas Edison, Alexander Graham Bell, Steve Jobs, and Bill Gates, have profoundly reshaped the world with their transformative contributions. These remarkable achievements raise a compelling question: What factors have led Americans to be exceptionally innovative compared to other nations? This study aims to explore the rich tapestry of American ingenuity, delving into contrasting examples that highlight the unique factors propelling American innovation to new heights.

The extensive catalog of inventions and industries created solely in America serves as a testament to the nation's innovation prowess. From McDonald's revolutionizing the fast-food industry to Starbucks transforming the culture of coffee consumption, American companies have left an indelible impact. Pioneers like Xerox revolutionized document reproduction, Henry Ford's Model T revolutionized transportation through mass production, and Google fundamentally altered information access. Facebook connected individuals across the globe, Hollywood brought captivating stories to life, and Amazon reshaped the retail landscape. Thomas Edison's electric power distribution system illuminated cities, while Spotify revolutionized music consumption. Boeing's innovations transformed air travel, fostering global connections. These diverse examples epitomize the breadth and depth of American innovation and entrepreneurship.

A striking contrast emerges when comparing the innovative landscape of America with that of other nations. Why did the birth of the airplane, the development of the lightbulb, the invention of the telephone, and the creation of the computer occur primarily in American rather than in the scientific hubs of Europe or other regions? Why has America been exceptionally innovative? These questions motivate the investigation of the historical, cultural, and socioeconomic factors that have shaped America's unparalleled spirit of innovation.

It is intriguing to contemplate how a relatively young nation like the United States has achieved extraordinary advancements. Despite Europe's possession of the oldest universities and Asia's rich history of ancient cultures, the United States has stand out as a hotbed of innovation. This study seeks to unravel the intricacies of this phenomenon, exploring how a nation with fewer centuries of history managed to surpass older civilizations in terms of groundbreaking inventions and pioneering industries. By closely examining the historical, cultural, and socioeconomic backdrop specific to the United States, this study aims to shed light on the unique elements that fostered an environment conducive to innovation and entrepreneurship.

1.1. Statement of the Problem

The emblematic examples of the airplane, lightbulb, telephone, and computer capture our imagination and serve as evidence that American innovation did not occur in isolation. These inventions were the result of a confluence of factors specific to the American context. When comparing the innovative landscape of America with that of other nations, a significant contrast emerges. This contrast generates curiosity and raises important questions regarding the factors that contribute to America's exceptional spirit of innovation.

The United States has acquired a well-deserved reputation as a nation of innovation, consistently spearheading groundbreaking inventions and pioneering industries. This reputation sparks a fundamental question: Why have Americans demonstrated exceptional levels of innovation compared to their counterparts in other nations? The remarkable achievements of American inventors and entrepreneurs throughout history call for an examination of the underlying factors that have propelled American innovation to unparalleled heights. Gaining a deeper understanding of these factors is essential to comprehend the roots of America's exceptional innovation culture.

The long list of inventions in the America reflect a broader historical, cultural, and socioeconomic context within the United States. To fully grasp the unique elements that have fostered an environment conducive to innovation and entrepreneurship, an exploration of the historical, cultural, and socioeconomic factors specific to the United States is necessary. Through this investigation, this study aims to explore the dynamic interplay of factors that have shaped America's exceptional spirit of innovation.

This study will examine the factors behind America's exceptional spirit of innovation. By delving into the fascinating historical business and technological successes, and intricate dynamics that have made the United States a cradle of invention and a beacon of entrepreneurial ingenuity, this study aims to understand the factors that set America apart. Through this inquiry, this study seeks to contribute to the academic understanding of innovation ecosystems and foster a deeper appreciation for the multifaceted factors that drive innovation within diverse cultural and societal contexts.

1.2. Research Objectives

A. Investigate the unique elements that fostered an environment conducive to innovation and entrepreneurship in America.

This study will explore the specific elements that have contributed to the creation of an environment in the United States that promotes innovation and entrepreneurship. By examining historical, cultural, and socioeconomic factors, this research aims to identify and analyze the key components that have played a crucial role in fostering innovation and entrepreneurial activities within the American context.

B. Examine the historical, cultural, and socioeconomic backdrop of the United States to gain deeper insights.
It is necessary to delve into the historical, cultural, and socioeconomic context of the United States for gaining a comprehensive understanding of the factors that have influenced and shaped American innovation. By examining the historical milestones, cultural values, and socioeconomic conditions that prevailed during pivotal periods of innovation, this research aims to provide a nuanced analysis of the interplay between these factors and their impact on the exceptional spirit of innovation in America.

C. Find out the factors that set America apart and contributed to its exceptional spirit of innovation.
In this study, there will be an effort to illuminate the specific factors that have distinguished the United States and contributed to its exceptional spirit of innovation compared to other nations. By exploring the contrasting examples of American innovation and comparing them with the intellectual landscapes of Europe, Asia, and other regions, this research aims to identify the unique elements that have propelled American innovation to unparalleled heights. By analyzing these factors, this study aims to deepen our understanding of the drivers behind America's remarkable innovative achievements.

Through these research objectives, this study endeavors to contribute to the academic discourse on innovation and entrepreneurship by shedding light on the distinct factors that have shaped America's exceptional spirit of innovation. By investigating the specific elements, examining the historical context, and analyzing the socioeconomic and cultural backdrop of the United States, this research aims to provide valuable insights into the dynamics that have fostered innovation and entrepreneurship within the American landscape.

1.3. Methodology

This study will employ a mixed-methods approach to gain a comprehensive understanding of the unique factors that have propelled American innovation. The methodology involves a synthesis of various research methods. Firstly, a comparative historical analysis will be conducted by reviewing relevant literature, and primary sources to examine the historical context, key events, policies, and societal changes influencing American innovation. A cultural and socioeconomic study will be conducted through ethnographic observations to explore the cultural values, social structures, and economic conditions fostering innovation in the United States. Cross-cultural comparisons will also be made. Comparative case studies will be selected to understand specific factors contributing to the success of significant American inventions and industries. By synthesizing these methods, this study aims to provide a comprehensive and nuanced exploration of the factors shaping American innovation.

1.4. Scope and Limitations

This study has specific scope and limitations that are outlined as follows:

- Geographic Focus:
The study will primarily focus on the United States and its historical, cultural, and socioeconomic context. It will not include an in-depth analysis of other countries such as Canada or South American countries. The aim is to narrow the scope

and concentrate on the unique factors within the American context that have contributed to innovation and entrepreneurship.

- Comparative Analysis with Europe:

When examining the historical aspects, the study will compare the findings with Europe, particularly after the 16th century. This comparative analysis will provide insights into the contrasting narratives of innovation and help contextualize the factors specific to the American innovation landscape.

- Critical Examination:

The study will adopt a critical approach and avoid solely applauding or celebrating American innovation. Instead, it will critically analyze the phenomena discovered during the research, evaluating their strengths, weaknesses, and potential implications. This critical examination aims to provide a balanced and objective understanding of the factors shaping American innovation.

It is important to acknowledge that these scope and limitations have been set to maintain focus and depth in the study. While the research primarily centers on the United States, it acknowledges the potential influence of external factors and invites critical evaluation to ensure a comprehensive analysis of American innovation.

1.5. Significance of the Study

This study holds significant importance as it aims to provide valuable insights into the factors that have propelled American innovation to unparalleled heights. The significance of this research can be understood in the following ways:

- *Gain deeper insights into the unique factors that propelled American innovation to unparalleled heights.*

By delving into the historical, cultural, and socioeconomic dynamics specific to the United States, this study will provide a comprehensive understanding of the factors that have played a pivotal role in fostering American innovation. Through this exploration, it will uncover the unique elements that have contributed to the exceptional spirit of innovation in the nation. The insights gained from this study will enhance our understanding of the foundations and drivers of American innovation, contributing to the broader knowledge of innovation ecosystems.

- *Understand the historical, cultural, and socioeconomic dynamics that contributed to America's exceptional spirit of innovation.*

The historical, cultural, and socioeconomic context of the United States has shaped its innovation landscape. By thoroughly examining these dynamics, this study will provide a deeper understanding of the factors that have influenced and contributed to America's exceptional spirit of innovation. It will shed light on the historical milestones, cultural values, and socioeconomic conditions that have created an environment conducive to innovation and entrepreneurship. Such understanding will not only illuminate the past but also offer insights into fostering innovation in the present and future.

- *Examine the contributions of American inventors and entrepreneurs warrant examination as they have significantly molded the contemporary world.*

This study will highlight and appreciate the remarkable achievements of these individuals, recognizing their transformative impact on various industries and sectors. By acknowledging their contributions, this research will contribute to a broader appreciation and recognition of the role played by American innovators in driving global progress.

- *Provide a basis for future research and exploration of innovation ecosystems in different countries.*

The findings and insights generated by this study will serve as a foundation for future research endeavors. The examination of the unique factors that have fueled American innovation can inspire further exploration of innovation ecosystems in different countries. By understanding the specific elements that have contributed to the success of American innovation, researchers can explore how these factors interact within different cultural, historical, and socioeconomic contexts, enriching the understanding of innovation on a global scale.

In conclusion, this study will provide deeper insights into the unique factors that have propelled American innovation, unravel the historical, cultural, and socioeconomic dynamics that have shaped America's exceptional spirit of innovation, appreciate the contributions of American inventors and entrepreneurs, and serve as a basis for future research and exploration of innovation ecosystems in different countries. Through these contributions, this research endeavors to advance the understanding of innovation and inspire further exploration in the field.

Achievers have an enabling attitude, realism, and a conviction that they themselves were the laboratory of innovation. Their ability to change themselves is central to their success. They have learned to conserve their energy by minimizing the time spent in regret or complaint. Every event is a lesson to them, every person a teacher.
Marilyn Ferguson

2. ENTREPRENEURSHIP AND INNOVATION

This part unveils a pivotal dimension within the United States' trajectory to global prominence. This section undertakes an in-depth analysis of the intrinsic significance of entrepreneurship and innovation within the American context, traversing historical foundations and contemporary ramifications. This scholarly inquiry entails a comprehensive review of pertinent literature, thereby elucidating the multifaceted rationales underpinning America's distinctive entrepreneurial vigor. Navigating the annals of American entrepreneurship history and crystallizing the essence of entrepreneurship and innovation are pivotal steps undertaken herein. Moreover, a critical examination of the interdependent relationship between entrepreneurship and innovation is presented, delineating the mutually propelling dynamics that characterize these phenomena. This academic exploration also dissects the profound implications of innovation on entrepreneurial attainment, thus illuminating the intricate forces that have engendered the multifarious American entrepreneurial landscape.

2.1. Background and significance of entrepreneurship and innovation in the US

The historical background of entrepreneurship and innovation in the United States stretches back to the earliest days of colonization.[1] When the first settlers arrived on American shores, they faced a challenging and uncertain environment, requiring a spirit of entrepreneurship and innovation to establish their new lives.

---

[1] Waterhouse, Benjamin C. *The land of enterprise: A business history of the United States.* Simon and Schuster, 2017.

The early settlers, such as the Pilgrims and Puritans, were driven by a spirit of religious freedom and economic opportunity. They relied on entrepreneurship and innovation to survive and thrive in a new and unfamiliar land. Through their resourcefulness, they developed new farming techniques, established trading networks, and built communities that laid the foundation for future economic growth.

As the colonies expanded, various industries emerged, each driven by entrepreneurial individuals seeking economic independence and prosperity. Agriculture played a vital role in the early economy, with entrepreneurs employing innovative farming methods, such as crop rotation and improved machinery.[2] The growth of trade and commerce led to the establishment of entrepreneurial ventures, including shipbuilding, fishing, and the development of trade routes. During the Revolutionary War and the formation of the new nation, entrepreneurship and innovation played a critical role. Founding fathers, such as Benjamin Franklin, exemplified the entrepreneurial spirit through their inventions, writings, and entrepreneurial endeavors.[3] Franklin's inventions, such as the lightning rod and bifocals, showcased American ingenuity and contributed to the advancement of scientific knowledge. The significance of entrepreneurship and innovation during this period was the establishment of a foundation that would shape the future of the nation. The entrepreneurial spirit demonstrated by early settlers and founding figures laid the groundwork for the values of individualism, self-reliance, and innovation that would become defining characteristics of American society.

---

[2] Bidwell, Percy Wells, and John Ironside Falconer. *History of agriculture in the northern United States, 1620-1860*. No. 358. Carnegie Institution of Washington, 1925.

[3] Brands, Henry William. *The first American: The life and times of Benjamin Franklin*. Anchor, 2010.

Entrepreneurship and innovation in the early years of American history were instrumental in shaping the country's economic and social fabric. The spirit of entrepreneurship fostered a culture of self-determination and risk-taking, creating an environment that encouraged individuals to pursue new ventures and push boundaries. These early entrepreneurial efforts established a foundation for the nation's economic growth, laying the groundwork for the transformative Industrial Revolution that would follow.

One of the defining periods in American history that propelled entrepreneurship and innovation was the Industrial Revolution.[4] During the late 18th and 19th centuries, technological advancements, such as the steam engine and the mechanization of production, revolutionized industries and fueled economic growth. Entrepreneurs like Andrew Carnegie, John D. Rockefeller, and Thomas Edison emerged as titans of industry, establishing massive corporations and driving innovation in sectors such as steel, oil, and electricity.[5]

The Gilded Age of the late 19th century and the early 20th century saw a surge in entrepreneurial activity, as individuals sought to capitalize on the expanding opportunities brought about by rapid industrialization and urbanization. This period witnessed the rise of innovative entrepreneurs like Henry Ford, who pioneered mass production techniques and transformed the automotive industry, and Alexander Graham Bell, whose invention of the telephone revolutionized communication.[6]

The 20th century witnessed a continuation of America's entrepreneurial spirit, with notable advancements in

---

[4] Teich, Mikulás, and Roy Porter, eds. *The industrial revolution in national context: Europe and the USA*. Cambridge University Press, 1996.

[5] Klein, Maury. *The change makers: from Carnegie to Gates, how the great entrepreneurs transformed ideas into industries*. Macmillan, 2003.

[6] Cashman, Sean Dennis. *America in the gilded age*. NYU Press, 1993.

technology, finance, and consumer goods. The emergence of Silicon Valley in California in the mid-20th century[7] marked a new era of technological innovation, as entrepreneurs like Steve Jobs, Bill Gates, and Mark Zuckerberg ushered in the digital revolution with the creation of companies like Apple, Microsoft, and Facebook.

The historical significance of entrepreneurship and innovation in the US is multifaceted. Economically, entrepreneurship has been a driving force behind job creation, economic growth, and the development of new industries. The entrepreneurial spirit has fueled competition, fostering a dynamic business environment that encourages efficiency and innovation. The US has consistently ranked as one of the most entrepreneurial countries globally, attracting talent, investment, and fostering a culture of innovation.

Moreover, entrepreneurship has had profound social and cultural impacts. It has been an avenue for social mobility, enabling individuals from diverse backgrounds to pursue their dreams and create wealth. Entrepreneurship has also been instrumental in shaping American society, driving advancements in fields such as healthcare, technology, entertainment, and beyond. In recent years, entrepreneurs have not only introduced groundbreaking products and services but have also challenged social norms, championed causes, and fostered inclusivity.

2.2. Literature Review: Exploring Diverse Explanations for American Entrepreneurship and Innovation

---

[7] Lécuyer, Christophe. *Making Silicon Valley: Innovation and the growth of high tech, 1930-1970.* MIT Press, 2006.

The growth and success of the United States in terms of entrepreneurship and innovation pose a fascinating puzzle that classical economic theories struggle to fully explain. While certain theories can shed light on specific stages or circumstances, there is no single theory that can comprehensively account for the remarkable three-hundred-year process of American growth. The initial attempts to explain American growth relied on the production factor theory, emphasizing the abundance of land, labor, and capital as driving forces. However, the availability of these resources alone does not explain the explosion of entrepreneurship witnessed in America but not in Europe, where similar resources were present. Other explanations, such as the abundance of natural resources or the influence of the Protestant work ethic, have also fallen short in providing a complete understanding. This chapter delves into the historical background and significance of entrepreneurship and innovation in the US, beginning with the first settlers and exploring various theories put forth by scholars to elucidate America's exceptional industrial development. By examining diverse perspectives, including those from Paul Kennedy, Jared Diamond, David Landes, Kate Pickett and Richard Wilkinson, Daron Acemoglu and James Robinson, and Noah Harari, this chapter seeks to uncover the complex factors that have shaped America's unique path to industrial prowess and shed light on why some countries excel more than others in terms of innovation and industry.

Classical economic theories cannot fully explain this growth. While certain theories can explain specific stages or situations, there is no single theory that can explain this three-hundred-year process. The first theory used to explain American growth was the production factor theory[8] found in ordinary economics textbooks. According to this theory, growth

---

[8] Mankiw, N. Gregory. *Principles of Economics*. 10th ed. Boston: Cengage, 2021. Print. p. 20.

---

occurred due to the abundance of land, labor, and capital. However, although all of these resources were also available in Europe, there was no explosion of entrepreneurship in Europe as there was in America.

The second explanation is based on the abundance of natural resources. However, these resources existed on the American continent before Christopher Columbus arrived, and the Native Americans did not utilize them for thousands of years. One of the most popular explanations is the Protestant work ethic. This explanation, introduced by Max Weber, claims that hard work and frugality lead to productivity and capital accumulation, and these moral values were also adopted by Americans from a religious perspective. It may be assumed that capital accumulation through hard work and thrift will lead to growth in an environment where natural resources, land, and labor are plentiful. However, such growth, leading to the creation of industry on a national scale, has not been observed in other areas of the world where Protestants are present. In America, society has created resources that are far beyond traditional resources. Additionally, American values are not solely created by using available natural resources through production and thrift. If that were the case, the natural resources would eventually become depleted. Americans are capable of producing new resources such as knowledge and technology beyond existing resources.

Economists generally divide the resources necessary for production into three main categories, as outlined in traditional economics textbooks: land, labor, and capital. However, over the past century, a fourth element has been added to the resources required for production: entrepreneurship.[9] Entrepreneurship is measured by the creative activities of individuals in an economy. Without

---

[9] Case, Karl E., Ray C. Fair, and Sharon M. Oster. *Principles of Economics.* 10th ed., NJ: Prentice Hall, 2012. p. 49.

entrepreneurship, an economy loses its ability to adapt to new conditions and lead innovation. Every economy, whether traditional or tightly regulated by laws as in a planned economy like China or a liberal economy like the US, requires entrepreneurs.

According to Peter Drucker, the primary activity of entrepreneurs is to create new opportunities.[10] Entrepreneurs develop technologies and organizations that were previously impossible. The industries and products that entrepreneurs create change our lives and what we do. For example, an entrepreneur brought together metal, plastic, and glass to produce automobiles. The resulting product, the automobile, changed not only our transportation habits but also our shopping habits and even where we live. Before automobiles, shopping was done at longer intervals focused on storage, but after automobiles, it became possible to shop more frequently. Additionally, automobiles enabled people to live further from the city center. The initiation of automobile production by an entrepreneur brought added prosperity to society. Therefore, all forms of entrepreneurship are critical to societal progress. Natural resources, capital, labor, and land can exist without entrepreneurs, but it is the entrepreneur who combines them to create added value and increase societal welfare.

While American society has produced some of the world's most significant entrepreneurs and industries that have shaped the 20th century, the question arises as to why fundamental industries did not emerge in Europe but did emerge in the US. There are numerous works of literature on the rise and fall of nations rather than on industries. One such

---

[10] Drucker, Peter F. *Innovation and Entrepreneurship: Practice and Principles*. New York: HarperBusiness, 1999. Print. p. 20.

work is Paul Kennedy's "The Rise and Fall of Great Powers,"[11] which attempts to explain the rise and fall of nations after the 15th century. Another work is Jared Diamond's "Guns, Germs, and Steel," [12] which examines why the US is wealthy while Papua New Guinea is poor and ultimately attributes the difference in development between countries to geographic advantage and the richness of natural resources. David S. Landes' "The Wealth and Poverty of Nations"[13] is another book that attempts to explain the wealth and poverty of nations through various parameters. A fourth source is Kate Pickett and Richard Wilkinson's book, "The Spirit Level."[14] Pickett and Wilkinson argue that high levels of income equality lead to the progress of a country. In contrast, it is noted that general development parameters are more negative in countries like the US, where the distance between the highest and lowest income brackets is high, compared to Japan or Scandinavian countries where income equality is higher. Noah Harari's book, "Sapiens, A Brief History of Humankind,"[15] delves into the progression of human societies and the influences that have shaped their growth. Harari's analysis highlights the vital role of the scientific revolution in sparking an era of innovation and shaping the trajectory of human progress.

---

[11] Kennedy, Paul M. *The Rise and Fall of the Great Powers: Economic Change and Military Conflict from 1500 to 2000.* New York: Random House, 1987.

[12] Diamond, Jared M. *Guns, Germs, and Steel: The Fates of Human Societies.* New York: W. W. Norton & Company, 1997.

[13] Landes, David S. *The Wealth and Poverty of Nations: Why Some Are So Rich and Some So Poor.* 1st ed. New York: W. W. Norton & Company, 1998.

[14] Pickett, Kate, and Richard Wilkinson. *The Spirit Level: Why More Equal Societies Almost Always Do Better.* London: Allen Lane, 2009.

[15] Harari, Yuval Noah. *Sapiens: A Brief History of Humankind.* New York: Harper Perennial, 2015.

One of the most notable works on the subject is "Why Nations Fail: The Origins of Power, Prosperity, and Poverty"[16] by Daron Acemoglu and James Robinson. The book attributes a nation's success or failure to democracy and democratic institutions. While autocratic regimes focus only on the interests of their close circles, democracies have institutions that work for the country's development and are successful in the long term.

Paul Kennedy attempts to explain the rise and fall of nations with a simplified model. Economically advanced nations are able to access military power, which gives them an advantage over other countries. In his book, he examines countries such as England, Germany, Russia, and the United States. When these countries progressed economically, they were able to advance militarily as well. Conversely, economic decline led to a decline in military power. However, a nation's rise or fall also has a comparative aspect. A country's position relative to its neighbors' economic power can determine whether that country rises or falls. When France and Germany both demonstrated economic progress, the country that showed greater economic progress would take over military and international political leadership. This model explains the United States' military power because it is natural for the world's largest economy to have a large military power. However, this model does not explain why the United States has industries that form the basis of a strong economy.

Jared Diamond defines the rise and fall of nations directly as a function of geography. In other words, countries grow according to the advantages and disadvantages brought about by their geographical position. For example, because there were animals such as sheep, cows, and chickens in Anatolia, agriculture based on these animals' products was possible.

---

[16] Acemoglu, Daron, and James A. Robinson. *Why Nations Fail: The Origins of Power, Prosperity, and Poverty*. New York: Crown, 2012.

However, in New Guinea, where these animals did not exist, agricultural production based on these animals' products did not develop historically or geographically. Only about 10 animals in the world can be used as a source of agricultural production (such as horses, cows, oxen, camels, sheep, goats, chickens, donkeys, buffaloes, etc.). The people living in areas where these animals exist were able to devote their time to producing cultural (knowledge-based products, iron-steel, ship, compass, weapons) products rather than agriculture. Writing developed in Mesopotamia, where almost all these animals lived. Although animals such as sheep, cows, and oxen did not exist in European geography, Europeans transported these animals to their continent and carried out agricultural production using them. When food supply became easier, time and opportunity arose to produce industrial tools and weapons. Weapons and economic power helped to provide an advantage over nations that did not possess these two things. Jared Diamond's geographic model can help explain America's economic development to a significant extent. Broad and fertile land, minerals, superiority in animal husbandry and agriculture, and the opportunity to benefit from all of Europe's written culture have been an advantage for development in America. However, despite having the same advantages, similar development as in America has not been achieved in South America or Europe. Therefore, this theory alone does not explain the development of America.

David Landes states that developing societies are those that can produce tools that allow production. He emphasizes that these societies can transform individual mastery knowledge into know-how that everyone can use in terms of knowledge management. He highlights that they can use people with expertise and competence in the right positions. He states that there is equality of opportunity for institutions and individuals in developing societies. Furthermore, he emphasizes that developing societies have rule of law that protects private property, individual liberties, and contracts much better than underdeveloped societies. Landes's analysis is also valid for the United States, which has achieved comparative progress.

Landes' analysis is not only relevant to the United States, but also to Europe, which has made comparable progress. However, his theories fail to explain why the US excels in industrial production. Kate Pickett and Richard Wilkinson argue that social inequality and income disparity within a country harm trust, increase depression and diseases, promote drug use, raise crime rates, teenage pregnancy, and obesity. A narrow gap between the lowest and highest income groups in a country results in positive developments in all the parameters listed. While these explanations define a country's level of development through its problems, it is more relevant to associate wealth with technology and brand production than a low obesity rate. Thus, Pickett and Wilkinson can explain why America has more drug addicts than Japan or Scandinavian countries, but not why it is a society that creates industry.

Daron Acemoğlu and James Robinson suggest that democratic institutions are essential for a country's development. Before the Arab Spring, the kings of North African countries were more concerned with their own and their close circles' welfare than their countries' development. Similarly, authoritarian regimes prioritize their own preservation and development all over the world. In democracies where power is distributed among institutions that can function, countries can develop. However, this theory cannot explain the development gap between America and other countries such as Scandinavian countries with democratic institutions.

In his book "A Brief History of Humankind," Noah Harari explores the evolution of human societies and the factors that have shaped their development. While not specifically focusing on industries, Harari's work offers insights into the broader patterns of human history that may shed light on the divergent paths of Europe and the US. His exploration of the cognitive revolution, agricultural revolution, and scientific revolution provides a framework for understanding the cultural and societal factors that have influenced innovation and economic growth.

None of the these works collectively explain America's innovative and industrial development. Kennedy's work highlights the relationship between economic and military power, Diamond's work is dependent on geography, and Landes associates industrialization with the rule set of a market economy. While Pickett and Wilkinson base their explanations on income inequality, Acemoğlu and Robinson attribute development to democratic institutions. After examining cultural, biological, geographic, political, and economic processes throughout history, all five works arrive at a model. While these works can explain why countries develop, they cannot explain why some developed countries excel more than others.

In addition to these works, there are books on business and entrepreneurship history. John Chamberlain's "The Enterprising Americans"[17] and Gerald Gusterson's "The Wealth Creators"[18] analyze American business and entrepreneurial history based on statistics and data. These two books provide important insights into the development of American entrepreneurship.

---

[17] Chamberlain, John. *The Enterprising Americans: A Chronicle of Business Enterprise.* New York: Harper & Brothers, 1963. Print.

[18] Gusterson, Gerald. *The Wealth Creators: The Rise of Venture Capital and the Fall of the Middle Class.* New York: Picador, 2017. Print.

John Chamberlain contends that American entrepreneurship developed because of the active role of the American state in business rather than passivity. The state and government system create a framework for the freedom of powers in a country. When the state places itself as an economic engine instead of free powers in the market, other market elements are uncertain. It is unclear whether resource distribution has any relation to individual needs when resources are allocated based on political will or social needs. Without the free movement of prices, profit margins, and wages, human preferences cannot be anticipated. America was founded in a new era with clear limits, but the pioneer who will exceed these limits is a free individual who walks on the horizon. Innovations by inventors, technicians, and companies are the primary reason for the rise in real wages. Investments have kept national income and total national production on a constantly rising trend. The contribution of the American business world and market economy goes beyond success in production.

The business system has enabled social cooperation among individuals and voluntary groups to a degree that cannot be achieved through central government planning. Without creative entrepreneurs in the business world, the ideal of freedom under the law would not have been realized. According to John Chamberlain, business is a process that eliminates class lines and directs individual effort towards consumer and public needs through the price-profit mechanism. Business is a creative pursuit within market rules that frees human labor and needs. In this sense, Chamberlain emphasizes that entrepreneurship can flourish in a free market economy.

In his book, Chamberlain highlights that the world is a changing and evolving field, implying that successful elements are those that are responsive to change, not cumbersome, flexible, and creative. Although the business process encompasses almost everyone, profit-seeking entrepreneurs have a critical role within all these elements. Profit is not just an added value obtained through labor, but a result of the entrepreneur taking risks by bringing together production factors. In a planned and static economy, where consumer demands and supply are fixed, there is no possibility of increasing profits or incurring losses. However, the American economy has never been static. Although every industry eventually reaches a limit, such as canals, toll roads, railway transportation, or whale oil trade, there have always been new ventures that create new demands and meet them. In other words, while kerosene was used for illumination during the Enlightenment, the invention of the light bulb eliminated the need for kerosene, but the automobile created a new need for petroleum, which is the main ingredient of kerosene.

American entrepreneurship is based on a free-market economy where every boundary encountered is surpassed, the playing field is expanded, the rules are set by the regulatory role of the state, no competition is entered into with players in the market, and entrepreneurship is based on a free market economy.

2.3. The Structure of American Entrepreneurship History

In the 1600s, it would have been unimaginable to predict that the American colonies would eventually become the world's most dominant power. At that time, the population of America was much smaller and incomparable to today's population, with only 200,000 people residing there. However, after the 1600s, America underwent a significant transformation. The population increased by a factor of 1,500, and the economic size of the country surpassed all other economies it could be compared with. The increase in production was even greater than the growth in population.

Today, the total annual production of colonial America can be generated in the first 15 minutes of a typical workday in America.[19]

When the first colonists arrived in the New World, there was no guidance program to assist them. Initially, scarcity of labor, money, and capital inspired their creativity. America's English roots allowed it to continue to acquire considerable technical knowledge from England without permission in the early 1800s. By 1906, however, the United States had made astonishing progress and became the world's largest producer in just two centuries.[20]

This growth in industrialization was made possible by small enterprises growing into large businesses and competition. Workshops in the iron and steel industry transformed into medium-sized factories and eventually large factories. The competition resulting from the emergence of companies through mergers and acquisitions also led to increased production and lower prices.

Although the monopolistic efforts in particular the petroleum industry in America led to some hesitation, anti-trust laws allowed new players to enter the market. Meanwhile, new technological products and services began to compete with old ones. Aluminum companies competed with wood and steel-producing companies. DuPont's nylon thread production provided an alternative to cotton, silk, and wool. Railroads faced competition from cars, trucks, and planes. Telephone and electrical systems were once entirely dependent on wires, but later, telephones and televisions began to function with wireless radio waves. Innovations in retail, such as

---

[19] Gerald Gunderson, *The Wealth Creators An Entrepreneurial History of the United States,* Truman Talley Books, 1989, s.1.

[20] Chamberlain, ibid, p. XIV.

supermarkets, and household appliances such as washing machines, dishwashers, and refrigerators, continued to emerge in a wide range.

Thus, the American experience became a success story. Americans inherited a rich continent with natural resources but left untapped from the Native Americans. Progress westward, expansion, and border extension shaped American institutions. While Americans were expanding their borders in the west, they moved forward without being dependent on the eastern government. In comparison, while the Russians were advancing in Siberia, they could not cut their ties to their then-capital. The Spaniards in South America, despite having similar rich and undeveloped areas as North Americans, could not achieve the success of the North Americans.

What determines the real boundaries of a country is the presence of creative individuals who seek to exceed limits in every field. ***When Americans refer to borders, they mean the line that needs to be crossed, whereas in South America, it means the point where they need to stop.*** In fact, two words in English reveal the essence of the matter. While "border" means edge and boundary, "frontier" comes from the word "front," meaning front or facade. "Frontier," derived from the word "front," is the point where a person moves forward when facing it. Therefore, Americans wanted to exceed limits in science, art, business, and every possible front. Americans owe much of their desire to move forward selectively to their European ancestors. By crossing the Atlantic Ocean, Americans left behind the king-subject, master-servant relationship, monarchical traditions, and a social system based on status and class.

When using English as a common language, Americans inherited English laws and Christianity's more liberating interpretations. The values that Americans and English people hold dear are those related to individual freedom and protection under the law, as established by Lord Coke[21] in the Magna Carta in the 16th century. Therefore, it was only natural for Americans to adopt John Locke's concept of "natural rights"[22] during the American Revolution.

A theory explaining the emergence of America should encompass the spirit of freedom and these traditions that were present on this continent, full of promises and opportunities. The Mercantilist movement[23] that emerged with the discoveries of the world, which aimed to capture the natural resources of the discovered countries, led to American rebellion against the British. Americans' evolving sense of freedom led them to resist the Mercantilist English, who wanted to exploit them and their natural resources.

Adam Smith's book "The Wealth of Nations,"[24] which argues that free-market economies are more beneficial and efficient for the societies they exist in, the American Declaration of Independence being published in the same year as the book and the adoption of both documents' values in America confirms the country's spirit of freedom. America's founders, who were highly knowledgeable in political philosophy, created a constitution that primarily protects individual political, religious, moral, and economic rights. They foresaw that economic and political freedom could coexist.

In America, the distribution of power among the federal government, states, and individual initiatives has been a

---

[21] Boyer, Allen D. *Sir Edward Coke and the Elizabethan Age*. Stanford University Press, 2003.

[22] Locke, John. "Natural rights." *Moral Reasoning: A Philosophic Approach to Applied Ethics, Dryden Press, London* (1990): 133-5.

[23] Heckscher, Eli F. *Mercantilism*. Routledge, 2013.

[24] Smith, Adam. *The wealth of nations [1776]*. Vol. 11937. na, 1937.

defining characteristic. Throughout history, the government has primarily focused on national defense, public safety, and the establishment of general laws, while leaving a significant portion of societal and economic development to the ingenuity and autonomy of individual and free institutions. This has played a pivotal role in establishing America as the cradle of entrepreneurship and innovation.

2.4. Definition: Entrepreneurship and Innovation

There have been many definitions of who an "Entrepreneur" is or what an entrepreneur do. Root of the word comes from French: "Entrepreneur-Entreprende" meaning "intermediary" or "go-between".

Definition of Entrepreneurship

Paul Burns[25] listed the meanings assigned to the word "entrepreneur" throughout history:

Middle Ages: A person who undertakes large-scale production projects
1600s: A person who takes a risk with the government to make a deal at a fixed price
1725: Richard Cantillon - A person who takes different risks from his/her capital
1803: John Bastist Say - A person who moves from a low productivity area to a high productivity area.
1876: Francis Walker - A person who earns profits from his/her managerial skills
1934: Joseph Schumpeter - An innovator who develops untested technologies
1975: Albert Shapero - A person who accepts the risk of making mistakes, organizes social and economic mechanisms, and takes initiative

---

[25] Paul Burns, *Entrepreneurship and Small Business*, Palgrave, London, 2001, s. 4.

1985: Robert Hisrich - A person who creates something of value, including financial, psychological, and social risks, with personal satisfaction and monetary reward, by devoting the necessary effort and time.

According to The Oxford English Dictionary, an entrepreneur is "a person who seeks to make a profit by taking risks and using initiative."

Despite these definitions, some questions remain unanswered. For instance, it is unclear whether a person who opens an ordinary coffee shop and someone who opens a coffee chain can both be considered entrepreneurs. The definitions above cannot provide a clear answer to the question of whether everyone who opens a shop is an entrepreneur. In his book "Entrepreneurship and Innovation," published in 1985, Peter Drucker says that entrepreneurs undertake four actions.[26] According to Peter Drucker, an entrepreneur is someone who maximizes opportunities, does the unexpected, does what should be done, does what is needed, and changes the structure of the market. Considering Peter Drucker's description, it becomes apparent that an entrepreneur is an individual who alters the structure of the market. For example, McDonald's created a fast-food industry by introducing the concept of "fast food" to the food market.

Entrepreneurs do the unexpected. While a particular innovation may not be demanded or expressed in society, the entrepreneur dreams of that innovation, works to bring it to light, and reveals it when conditions permit. For example, before Facebook was introduced, no one was demanding a social network called "Facebook." Mark Zuckerberg imagined this social network and eventually brought it to light.

---

[26] Peter Drucker, ibid. p. 23.

Entrepreneurs do what should be done. Entrepreneurs do what everyone else is doing when conditions allow for a new leap. To be successful, an entrepreneur must have conditions that are conducive to a new leap. For example, while the disadvantages of gas lamps and the fires they caused were evident, Thomas Edison, an entrepreneur, tried to produce a light source that was safer, more easily accessible, cost-effective, and efficient.

Entrepreneurs do what is needed. For an entrepreneur to be successful in the market, there must be a need for the new product to be introduced. For example, when transportation needs increased, cars were quickly accepted by society when they were introduced to the market. The reason why trains or railroads developed more in America is due to the enormity of the transportation needs in America.

Entrepreneurs change the structure of the market. Whatever product or service the entrepreneur brings, it changes the way a particular need is met in an unparalleled way compared to the past.

The advent of the internet has eliminated almost entirely the classic form of personal letter writing and has given rise to a completely new market or industry in communication. Social media and communication tools such as Hotmail, Twitter, Facebook, and WhatsApp have also fundamentally changed the structure of traditional communication markets.
Turning to the question of whether a person who opens a hamburger stand and a person who creates a hamburger chain can be classified as entrepreneurs, according to Peter Drucker, the answer is not just the person who opens the hamburger stand. When a hamburger stand is opened, nothing new is created; it is simply copied from something that has been done before. However, when a hamburger chain like McDonald's is created, a venture that changes the structure of the market is

undertaken. Nonetheless, the underlying reason why someone who opens a food stand or a hamburger shop may be referred to as an "entrepreneur" by society is perhaps because very few people have the courage to take the risk and start a commercial enterprise or launch a venture when most people choose to work for someone else.

In this study, entrepreneurship will be approached in the sense defined by Peter Drucker because his definition of entrepreneurship results in the creation of an industry.

Gunderson[27] identified three characteristics of an entrepreneur:

The first characteristic of an entrepreneur is the drive to realize their own dreams with a unique passion. The effort to realize their vision inherently involves creativity in producing something that does not yet exist.

The second characteristic of entrepreneurship is to identify and capitalize on an opportunity that others may not have noticed or ignored. What may be a problem for many people can be an opportunity for an entrepreneur. For example, while heart disease may be a problem for many people, for an entrepreneur who manufactures drugs, it is an opportunity.

The third characteristic of entrepreneurship is working persistently to realize their own ideas.

It can be argued that the entrepreneurs who have created industries in America possess these three characteristics identified by Gunderson. American entrepreneurs have pursued their dreams, seen problems as opportunities, and worked persistently to achieve their goals, even in the face of all obstacles.

---

[27] Gunderson, ibid, p.7.

Based on these evaluations, it can be said that entrepreneurs are a critical resource for many countries around the world because they are the driving force behind the development of a nation. However, some American entrepreneurs, following Peter Drucker's definition, have assumed the role of entrepreneurship in a way that differs from the rest of the world and created industries through innovation. The American entrepreneur, characterized by the American context, has had the opportunity to create industries by innovating.

2.5. The relationship between entrepreneurship and innovation

Understanding the relationship between entrepreneurship and innovation is essential for comprehending the dynamics of economic growth and societal progress. While entrepreneurship refers to the process of identifying and seizing opportunities to create and manage ventures, innovation involves the introduction of new ideas, products, services, or processes that bring about positive change. These two concepts are interconnected and mutually reinforcing. Entrepreneurs, driven by their vision, creativity, and risk-taking mindset, are catalysts for innovation, as they envision and bring to life new ideas and solutions. At the same time, innovation fuels entrepreneurship by creating opportunities for entrepreneurs to identify unmet needs, disrupt existing industries, and generate economic value. Together, entrepreneurship and innovation foster economic development, job creation, and social advancement. By studying the intricate relationship between entrepreneurship and innovation, researchers, policymakers, and practitioners gain insights into the drivers, mechanisms, and outcomes of transformative change in societies and economies. This understanding can inform the design of supportive ecosystems, policies, and strategies to foster a thriving entrepreneurial and innovative culture that drives sustainable growth and prosperity.

One notable example of the symbiotic relationship between entrepreneurship and innovation in the US is the rise of Silicon Valley.[28] Starting in the mid-20th century, a cluster of technology companies emerged in the San Francisco Bay Area, fueling unprecedented innovation in the field of information technology. Entrepreneurs such as Steve Jobs and Steve Wozniak, co-founders of Apple Inc., and Bill Gates, co-founder of Microsoft Corporation, pioneered the development of personal computers and revolutionized the way people interact with technology. Their entrepreneurial vision and drive for innovation laid the foundation for the digital revolution, shaping the modern world and paving the way for advancements in computing, communication, and entertainment.

Another compelling example is the success of innovative startups in sectors like biotechnology and healthcare. The US has witnessed the emergence of numerous entrepreneurial ventures that have revolutionized medical treatments, diagnostics, and healthcare delivery. Companies like Genentech, Amgen, and Moderna have transformed the landscape of biotechnology and pharmaceuticals, introducing breakthrough therapies and vaccines that have saved countless lives and improved global health outcomes.[29] These entrepreneurial endeavors have not only driven scientific

---

[28] Lewis, Michael M. *The new new thing: A Silicon Valley story*. WW Norton & Company, 2000.

[29] Freyer, F. F., & Saltzman, J. (2020, May 19). 'This is not how you do science': Cambridge biotech Moderna's potential COVID-19 vaccine stirs hope — and criticism. The Boston Globe. Retrieved from https://www.bostonglobe.com/2020/05/19/business/hope-covid-19-vaccine-attracts-investors-cambridge-biotech/

advancements but also stimulated economic growth and job creation.

The entertainment industry in the US is another vivid illustration of the close relationship between entrepreneurship and innovation. Hollywood, the epicenter of the global film and television industry, has consistently produced groundbreaking films, TV shows, and digital content that captivate audiences worldwide. Entrepreneurs, producers, directors, and artists have pushed the boundaries of storytelling, visual effects, and immersive experiences, leading to the emergence of new technologies, distribution platforms, and business models. This blend of entrepreneurial spirit and innovative creativity has propelled the American entertainment industry to be a dominant force globally, shaping popular culture and generating substantial economic value.

However, it is important to note that the entertainment industry is not without its challenges. Uncertainty in the movie industry, for example, is a significant factor that entrepreneurs and investors must contend with. The success of a film at the box office is often unpredictable, and factors such as star power and marketing efforts can influence its performance This uncertainty can make it difficult for entrepreneurs to make informed decisions and can impact the financial viability of projects. Despite these challenges, the entrepreneurial and innovative nature of the American entertainment industry has allowed it to thrive and remain at the forefront of global entertainment. The industry continues to evolve, with new technologies and business models constantly emerging. As a result, the American entertainment industry will likely continue to shape popular culture and generate substantial economic value in the future.

Furthermore, the US has a long history of fostering entrepreneurial ecosystems that encourage innovation across various sectors. The foundation of prestigious research institutions like Stanford and MIT has been crucial in fostering an atmosphere that supports innovation and the exchange of knowledge.[30] These institutions have acted as catalysts for entrepreneurship, providing aspiring entrepreneurs with access to cutting-edge research, mentorship, and funding opportunities. The presence of venture capital firms and angel investors in cities like Silicon Valley and Boston has further facilitated the growth and success of innovative startups, enabling them to scale their operations, attract talent, and bring transformative ideas to market.

In conclusion, the United States exemplifies the intricate relationship between entrepreneurship and innovation. Through the stories of Silicon Valley, biotechnology startups, the entertainment industry, and thriving entrepreneurial ecosystems, it becomes evident that entrepreneurial vision, combined with innovative thinking, has been the driving force behind the nation's remarkable achievements. The entrepreneurial spirit and culture of innovation in the US have continually sparked advancements in technology, healthcare, entertainment, and beyond, contributing to economic growth, societal progress, and a lasting impact on the global stage.

2.6. Examining the impact of innovation on entrepreneurial success

Innovation and entrepreneurship are inextricably linked[31], with innovation serving as a catalyst for entrepreneurial success. The United States has long been recognized as a global leader in entrepreneurship, fostering an environment

---

[30] Prokop, Daniel. "University entrepreneurial ecosystems and spinoff companies: Configurations, developments and outcomes." Technovation 107 (2021): 102286.

[31] Farinha, Luís, João JM Ferreira, and Sara Nunes. "Linking innovation and entrepreneurship to economic growth." Competitiveness Review: An International Business Journal 28.4 (2018): 451-475.

that encourages and rewards innovation. This essay aims to delve into the impact of innovation on entrepreneurial success within the context of the US. Through the examination of noteworthy case studies, industry trends, and pivotal drivers of innovation, valuable insights will be derived into how innovation has molded the entrepreneurial terrain and added to the economic well-being of the nation.

To comprehend the impact of innovation on entrepreneurial success, it is essential to establish a clear understanding of innovation in the context of entrepreneurship. Innovation can take various forms, including product innovation, process innovation, and business model innovation.[32] Each type of innovation plays a unique role in driving entrepreneurial ventures forward, fueling growth, and establishing competitive advantages. Successful entrepreneurs recognize the power of innovation to disrupt existing industries, create new markets, and generate sustainable business growth.

Innovation empowers entrepreneurs with a distinct competitive edge in the marketplace.[33] Through the development and implementation of innovative ideas, technologies, and strategies, entrepreneurs can revolutionize industries and capture significant market share. Numerous case studies highlight the transformative impact of innovative startups on their respective industries. For instance, the introduction of ride-sharing platforms like Uber and Lyft revolutionized the transportation sector, challenging traditional taxi services and transforming the way people commute. This demonstrates how innovation can disrupt

---

[32] Keeley, Larry, et al. Ten types of innovation: The discipline of building breakthroughs. John Wiley & Sons, 2013.

[33] Berawi, Mohammed Ali. "Quality revolution: leading the innovation and competitive advantages." International Journal of Quality & Reliability Management 21.4 (2004): 425-438.

established industries and pave the way for entrepreneurial success.

The United States has nurtured a supportive environment for innovation, driven by various factors. First, substantial investments in research and development (R&D) play a pivotal role in driving innovation. Both government funding and corporate R&D initiatives contribute to the advancement of cutting-edge technologies and the creation of innovative solutions. Additionally, vibrant entrepreneurial ecosystems facilitate innovation by providing access to capital, supportive regulatory frameworks, networking opportunities, and mentorship programs. Notable startup hubs like Silicon Valley, Boston, and Austin exemplify the power of entrepreneurial ecosystems in fostering innovation and driving entrepreneurial success.[34]

Innovation permeates key industries in the US, propelling entrepreneurial ventures and shaping their success. The technology and information technology (IT) sector has been a breeding ground for innovation, with groundbreaking advancements in artificial intelligence, blockchain, and the Internet of Things. Startups such as Airbnb, which disrupted the hospitality industry, and Netflix, which revolutionized the entertainment industry, exemplify the impact of innovation in technology-driven entrepreneurship. Similarly, the healthcare and biotechnology sectors have witnessed significant innovation, leading to the development of breakthrough therapies, medical devices, and digital health solutions. These innovations have not only improved patient outcomes but also created new entrepreneurial opportunities.

---

[34] Geibel, Richard C., and Meghana Manickam. "Comparison of selected startup ecosystems in Germany and in the USA Explorative analysis of the startup environments." GSTF Journal on Business Review (GBR) 4.3 (2016).

Renewable energy and sustainability have also emerged as critical areas for innovation in the US. Entrepreneurs are driving innovation in clean energy technologies, smart grids, and sustainable solutions to address environmental challenges.[35] By leveraging innovative approaches, entrepreneurs contribute to the transition to a greener economy and the creation of new business opportunities. Successful renewable energy startups have demonstrated how innovation can foster environmental sustainability while driving entrepreneurial success.

While innovation presents immense opportunities, it also comes with challenges for entrepreneurs. Protecting intellectual property rights is crucial to incentivize innovation; however, entrepreneurs often face obstacles in safeguarding their innovations. Robust intellectual property frameworks are essential to ensure that entrepreneurs can reap the benefits of their innovative ideas and technologies. Collaborative innovation, involving partnerships between different stakeholders, can also enhance entrepreneurial success by leveraging diverse expertise and resources. Open innovation platforms, industry-academia collaborations, and innovation networks facilitate knowledge sharing and collaborative problem-solving.

The examination of the impact of innovation on entrepreneurial success in the US highlights the vital role of innovation in driving economic growth, job creation, and societal advancements.

---

[35] Bell, James, and Jelmer Stellingwerf. "Sustainable entrepreneurship: The motivations and challenges of sustainable entrepreneurs in the renewable energy industry." (2012).

It was wonderful to find America, but it would have been more wonderful to miss it.
Mark Twain

3. UNIFYING AMERICAN VALUES AND ELEMENTS THAT MAKE AMERICA ENTREPRENEURIAL AND INNOVATIVE

The United States is a country that came into being due to a unique set of historical conditions. This set of conditions has also shaped the mindset of the country, resulting in the emergence of the American mindset. The American mindset not only nurtures entrepreneurship but has also paved the way for the establishment of the world's largest industries. This mindset has arisen as a result of the interplay of various distinct American phenomena. This section of the study will explore the historical context in which American entrepreneurship emerged and the factors that have molded the American entrepreneurial mindset.

In this study, the term "context" refers to a specific set of conditions under which an event, idea, or term can be understood and evaluated holistically. The American mindset can be comprehended within a particular set of conditions unique to the United States. The American context differs from many other countries and regions that share similar size. America's development has occurred in a different set of circumstances than China, Russia, India, South America, and Europe. Although America shares a few similarities with some of these countries, such as natural resources, multiculturalism, and geographic size, it differs from them in many other respects. Additionally, in a process where most inputs are different, even a few similar inputs can function entirely differently and lead to different outcomes.

This study aims to examine the reasons and examples of how the minds of entrepreneurs who shape the world by creating industries were shaped by the American context, the conditions unique to America, and how the American mindset emerged. While the focus of the study is on America, reference will also be made to continental Europe and European countries. Why have the world's largest industries emerged not in the mature and old continent of Europe, which experienced the Enlightenment, the Renaissance, and the French Revolution, but in the new world of America? In this study, comparisons between America and European countries, like some of the authors referenced, will be made to better understand America and its context.

The unique conditions that set the United States apart from other countries and the characteristics of the American context are listed below. In this section, a brief overview is provided to show the whole picture of the conditions. Later, each feature will be explained in greater detail with more extensive references.

The Unifying American Values that shape the American Entrepreneurial Spirit can be categorized into three main groups and the subheadings listed below:

The Unifying American Values and Elements that Shape the American Entrepreneurial Spirit
Pushing Beyond the Borders (Frontierism)
• Pioneering
• Creativity and Innovation
• Taking Risks
• Competition and Renewal

American Individualism
• Social Structure Based on Meritocracy
• American Dream
• American Individualism

• Self-Made Man

Unique Historical, Religious, Philosophical, and Legal
Elements of America
• The Melting Pot
• Protestant Work Ethic
• Pragmatism
• Existence of Property and Intellectual Property Rights

The unifying American values and elements that form the
American entrepreneurial spirit can be examined in three
main categories: Beyond the Frontier Drive, American
Individualism, and Unique American Philosophical,
Religious, Historical, and Legal Elements.

The Beyond the Frontier Drive constitutes the fundamental
dynamism of entrepreneurship in America, driven by the
effort to go where no one has gone before and do what has
never been done before. This category includes concepts such
as Pioneer Spirit, Creativity and Innovation, Risk-Taking,
Competition, and Renewal.

American Individualism is at the core of American
entrepreneurship. The unique American individualism
mindset of self-made success, where individuals can create
something out of nothing and the belief that meritorious
people can rise in society and organizations, has provided a
foundation for American entrepreneurship.

Unique American philosophical, religious, historical, and legal
elements have also shaped American entrepreneurship.
Pragmatism has become the most distinctive philosophy of
the American business world. Protestant work ethic is the
primary religious understanding behind the hard work and
productivity of American entrepreneurs. The concept of the
Melting Pot has also been a critical element in distinguishing
American entrepreneurs from their counterparts in other

countries. People from different ethnic backgrounds and cultures have worked to develop both themselves and the country they call home. Legal conditions have also played a role in the success of American entrepreneurship, with property rights and intellectual property rights being established early and becoming tradable, providing significant opportunities for American entrepreneurs.

The integration of these values into American society has brought about an entrepreneurial spirit that has led to industry and innovation. The unique American philosophical, religious, historical, and legal elements have provided a foundation for the emergence of the entrepreneurial spirit in America. Each of these categories is explained below.

3.1. Introduction

The United States of America is synonymous with opportunity and has long stood as a beacon for innovation and entrepreneurial pursuits. The exceptional flair for innovation and robust entrepreneurial spirit of the nation stem from a multifaceted amalgamation of values, historical contexts, and cultural components. This examination seeks to unravel the cohesive American values and elements that mold the entrepreneurial spirit of the nation, bestowing upon it a distinctive and dynamic essence that has intrigued the global imagination.

Before delving into the details of 'The Unifying American Values and Elements that Shape the American Entrepreneurial Spirit,' a concise explanation of each value and element will be provided in this introductory chapter. This will allow readers to gain a holistic view and an initial insight into these components.

Pioneering:

Central to the American narrative is the essence of pioneering, a defining element since the nation's inception. This is not just limited to territorial expansions but symbolizes a resolute dedication to exploring uncharted territories and redefining possibilities. This spirit of pioneering is evident in the relentless quest for new concepts, industries, and advancements, acting as a catalyst for innovation and entrepreneurship.

Creativity and Innovation:

Creativity and innovation constitute the essence of American entrepreneurship, with the nation being the birthplace of numerous groundbreaking inventions. It creates an environment conducive to the generation of revolutionary ideas and applauds risk and experimentation. This culture of innovation is the engine propelling the nation's transformative impact on industries and the world.

Taking Risks:

The propensity to undertake risks is integral to entrepreneurship in the United States. The national history is marked by bold endeavors in diverse fields such as business, science, and exploration. Embracing risks, often inspired by the allure of the American Dream, is fundamental to the country's entrepreneurial ethos, enabling individuals to confront and overcome uncertainties, emerging more resilient.

Competition and Renewal:

The competitive ecosystem and the free-market structure have been pivotal in catapulting the nation into a global innovation leader. This relentless aspiration to excel fosters industrial evolution and continuous reinvention, positioning innovation at the core of economic advancement. This relentless pursuit of excellence enhances the country's entrepreneurial vibrancy.

Social Structure Based on Meritocracy:
The American society uniquely upholds meritocracy, recognizing and rewarding talent, diligence, and ambition over inherited status. This principle permeates the entrepreneurial landscape, promoting an inclusive environment where accomplishments are valued and diverse backgrounds are embraced.

American Dream:
The notion of the American Dream, representing the promise of a better life through hard work and ingenuity, has attracted myriad individuals to the nation. It has motivated generations of entrepreneurs to relentlessly pursue their visions, serving as a symbol of hope and opportunity.

American Individualism:
The ethos of American individualism emphasizes personal liberty and self-sufficiency, enabling individuals to carve their destinies and pursue their entrepreneurial aspirations independently, thereby contributing to societal progress.

Self-Made Man:
The ideal of the self-made man exemplifies American entrepreneurship, symbolizing the potential for individuals to ascend from modest beginnings to attain substantial achievements through their own endeavors. Iconic entrepreneurs exemplify this ideal, serving as a source of inspiration for others to realize their potential to reshape their destinies and impact the world.

The Melting Pot:
The convergence of diverse cultures, ideologies, and backgrounds in America has birthed the concept of the melting pot, a space where diversity is valued, and the fusion of varied viewpoints catalyzes innovation. This cultural convergence creates a fertile environment conducive to entrepreneurial flourishing.

Protestant Work Ethic:

The Protestant Work Ethic, originating from the values of early European settlers, underscores the virtues of hard work, discipline, and diligence. This ethic has profoundly shaped the American perspective on work and entrepreneurship, fostering a dedication to industriousness and persistence.

Pragmatism:

The philosophical disposition of pragmatism in America prioritizes practical solutions and efficient problem-solving. This approach has steered the creation of innovative products, services, and industries, reflecting the practical and solution-oriented mindset of American entrepreneurs.

Existence of Property and Intellectual Property Rights:

The assurance of property and intellectual property rights protection is foundational to the American legal framework. It gives entrepreneurs the assurance to innovate, secure in the knowledge that their intellectual creations will be protected, nurturing a domain where creativity and invention can thrive unrestricted.

In the ensuing sections, each of these components will undergo a meticulous examination.

When America's early pioneers first turned their eyes toward the West, they did not demand that somebody take care of them if they got ill or got old. They did not demand maximum pay for minimum work, and even pay for no work at all.
Paul Harvey

3.1.1 *Pioneerism*

In 1893, American historian Frederick Jackson Turner introduced the "Frontier Thesis," which reflects one of the important character traits of Americans.[36] According to this thesis, Americans who migrated from various parts of the world tried to go beyond the existing boundaries in every field with their discovery and pioneering spirit while cutting their ties with traditions. The westward expansion of settlement on the eastern coast of America is explained by Turner's "Frontier Thesis." Today, the Frontier Thesis is not only about constantly pushing geographical boundaries, but also about pushing scientific, artistic, and technological boundaries. Many technological inventions have been made possible by taking scientific boundaries a step further in America. Similarly, the effort to go beyond the known boundaries in the field of art has allowed for the emergence of innovations.

The pioneer concept includes those who represent movements and ideas that bring about change in social systems or organizations. While pioneering was synonymous with discovery before the 20th century, the word "pioneering" began to be associated with innovation in the 20th century and beyond, particularly in the field of technology. This is because pioneers, especially in the field of technology, began to produce innovation.

In American history, pioneers were people who developed settlement areas from east to west. The pioneer label was especially given to the first immigrants who went to areas that had not been settled before. These people wanted to create a permanent settlement system by going to areas that had never been stepped on before in order to establish a new life.

---

[36] Frederick Jackson Turner, The Significance of the Frontier in American History, Penguin Great Ideas, 2008.

The effort to go beyond the boundaries, in practice, meant that pioneer communities protected themselves from all kinds of danger, utilized the land efficiently, and established an economy and market that would sustain their lives.

Although the effort to go beyond the frontier is often considered an individual effort, the struggle against nature, natives, and climate led pioneers to form communities by working together in different regions. These communities can also be considered the beginnings of towns, cities, and states.

In this sense, American pioneers established farms, defense systems, legal systems, and city systems. Thanks to these systems, pioneering has meant providing a way of life not only for themselves but also for future generations.

Within the pioneer concept, cowboys, hunters, prospectors, and miners who went beyond the boundaries of settlement areas hold an important place in American literature and culture.

The Gold Rush is another historical reality of American pioneering. The gold rush movement in America always follows a typical pattern. Firstly, a pioneer finds gold in a specific location. The pioneer separates the gold he found from the sand and gravel with primitive methods. The news of the gold discovery attracts other pioneers to the area like a magnet, and thus, a process of searching for gold and cleaning found gold begins.[37]

If it is discovered that the found gold mine is a large deposit, then companies that provide gold mining and separation services from other materials begin to arrive. The previously

[37] Holub, Joan, and H. Q. Who. What was the Gold Rush?. Penguin, 2013.

untouched natural area suddenly becomes the center of mining, transportation, food, drink, and accommodation establishments that serve pioneers and prospectors. Thus, a movement that begins with a pioneer leads to the complete settlement of a particular region. The reasons behind the Gold Rush phenomenon are clearly personal enrichment.

The effort to go beyond the frontier, which has been integrated with pioneers, continued from the colonial period to the 20th century and beyond, manifested itself in many fields, especially in geography and economic development. After the end of geographical discoveries, pioneering emerged in the fields of science and technology. Examples of pioneering can be seen in many fields, from electric appliances to airplanes.

The story of the Wright Brothers' invention of the airplane also provides clues to the characteristics of pioneering. Wilbur and Orville Wright, two bicycle mechanics from Dayton, Ohio, began systematically studying everything that could give them clues about how birds fly in 1890. The Wright Brothers quickly realized that there was nothing in scientific works or the experiences of ancient people that could be useful to them. In other words, they had to be pioneers in finding a flying method other than wing flapping. They fixed the wings on a stable system and used a propeller attached to an engine to create the airflow generated by wing flapping. The only thing they learned from birds was the slight angles they gave to their wings to steer themselves while gliding. This allowed the Wright Brothers to go beyond the boundaries. All of this was the technical part of the job. Although the Wright Brothers were the first to create a flying machine in the world, they also wanted the pride of succeeding in this endeavor and the financial gains that came with it.[38] [39]Personal gain was also behind pioneering, in addition to scientific curiosity.

Therefore, pioneering is not just about bravely venturing into the unknown; it is about establishing a life system in an unexplored environment. The most interesting aspect of pioneering is the collective support of individual interests. Although pioneering is an individual endeavor, the safety and survival of a pioneer depend on the support of other people. Especially in environments where any vital support is not available, pioneers are dependent on the support of other pioneers. They need to collaborate to meet many of their needs, such as food, shelter, transportation, money storage, and protection. Therefore, pioneers have established a natural division of labor where they set up a bar-restaurant for food needs, a grocery store for shopping needs, a bank for money storage and withdrawal needs, a school for education needs, and a bank for security needs. This microscopic level of cooperation initially helped build a civilization in the remote West.

3.1.1.1. Criticism to American Pioneerism
American pioneerism has been celebrated as a key factor in the success of entrepreneurship in the United States, but there are also critical perspectives to this phenomenon that should be examined.

One perspective is that American pioneerism is often romanticized and overlooks the displacement and marginalization of indigenous communities. The westward expansion in the 19th century, which is often seen as a

---

[38] Orville Wright, Rupert Holland, The Story of the Wright Brothers and the Flying Machine, Cornell Publications, 2011.

[39] Garrett, Leslie. DK Readers L4: First Flight: The Story of the Wright Brothers. Penguin, 2012.

triumph of American pioneerism, involved the forced removal of Native American communities from their ancestral lands.[40] This displacement not only had devastating consequences for those communities but also paved the way for American settlers to establish new businesses and industries.

Another critical perspective is that American pioneerism can lead to a "winner-takes-all" mentality, where the pursuit of individual success comes at the expense of the collective good. This perspective can be seen in the rise of monopolies in industries such as oil, steel, and railroads during the late 19th and early 20th centuries. While these monopolies brought great wealth to their owners, they also stifled competition and innovation, which ultimately hurt consumers and smaller businesses.[41]

A third perspective is that American pioneerism can be exclusionary and reinforce existing power structures. For example, while the American Dream of upward mobility and success is often held up as a key tenet of American pioneerism, it has not been equally accessible to all Americans. Historical examples of exclusionary practices include racial segregation and discrimination in hiring and lending practices.[42] These practices have prevented many people from fully realizing their entrepreneurial potential and contributing to the economy.

---

[40] Jacobs, Margaret D. White mother to a dark race: Settler colonialism, maternalism, and the removal of Indigenous children in the American West and Australia, 1880-1940. U of Nebraska Press, 2009.

[41] Loewen, James W. Lies my teacher told me: Everything your American history textbook got wrong. The New Press, 2008.

[42] Franklin, John Hope. "History of racial segregation in the United States." The ANNALS of the American Academy of Political and Social Science 304.1 (1956): 1-9.

Despite these critical perspectives, it is important to acknowledge that American pioneerism has also played a positive role in entrepreneurship. The belief in the power of individual initiative and creativity has led to many groundbreaking innovations and advancements in technology, medicine, and other fields. For example, Thomas Edison, who was self-taught and came from a low-income family, was able to develop and patent over 1,000 inventions throughout his lifetime.[43]

Moreover, the spirit of American pioneerism has also fostered a culture of risk-taking and innovation that has encouraged entrepreneurship and economic growth. The development of Silicon Valley, which is home to some of the world's most innovative and successful tech companies, is a prime example of the entrepreneurial spirit that has been fueled by American pioneerism.

In conclusion, while American pioneerism has been a driving force behind the success of entrepreneurship in the United States, it is important to also critically examine the negative consequences that it can have. By recognizing and addressing these issues, the research can proceed towards creating a more inclusive and equitable environment for all entrepreneurs to thrive and contribute to the economy.

3.1.1.2. Pioneerism in Europe
The concept of pioneerism has played a crucial role in American history and culture. American pioneers were individuals who ventured into new territory and established permanent settlement systems. The idea of pushing boundaries and going beyond the limits has been an important characteristic of American society, and it has led to

[43] Barnham, Kay. Thomas Edison. Capstone Classroom, 2014.

the development of various fields, such as science, art, and technology.

However, it is interesting to note that Europe did not have a similar type of pioneerism in continental Europe between 1600 and now. One of the main reasons for this difference can be attributed to the geographical and historical context. Unlike the United States, Europe had a long history of civilization and urbanization dating back to the Roman Empire. By the 1600s, much of Europe was already densely populated, and the land was largely cultivated and settled.

Additionally, the political and social structures in Europe were already established, with existing legal, economic, and administrative systems. There was less of a need for pioneers to establish new systems from scratch, as these structures were already in place. Moreover, Europe had a more rigid social hierarchy and a stronger sense of tradition and conservatism, which made it harder for individuals to break away from the established norms and values.

Furthermore, Europe had already gone through a period of exploration and expansion in the 15th and 16th centuries with the discovery of the New World, Asia, and Africa. European nations had already established colonies and trading posts in these regions, which allowed them to expand their influence and power globally.[44] This expansion was driven by economic and political interests, and it did not require the same level of individual initiative and innovation as American pioneerism.

In conclusion, while the concept of pioneerism has played a significant role in American history and culture, it is not a universal phenomenon that can be found in all regions and contexts. The differences between American and European

---

[44] Magnusson, Lars. Routledge Explorations in Economic History: Political Economy of Mercantilism. Taylor & Francis, 2015.

historical, geographical, social, and political contexts have resulted in distinct patterns of development and innovation.

Creativity is just connecting things. When you ask creative people how they did something, they feel a little guilty because they didn't really do it, they just saw something. It seemed obvious to them after a while. That's because they were able to connect experiences they've had and synthesize new things.
Steve Jobs

3.1.2. Creativity and Innovation

One of the reasons why the United States is considered the leading country in creativity and innovation is the numerous inventors, entrepreneurs, and businessmen who have emerged from the country, including Graham Bell, Edison, the Wright Brothers, Henry Ford, and Steve Jobs. One factor that has contributed to the prominence of business creativity in America is the innovative efforts made to address the country's needs. For example, the development of the telephone, the automobile, and the computer, all of which emerged as a result of the country's communication, transportation, and data processing needs, respectively.

To move these inventions into mass production, other technologies were required, and each invention also triggered the development of other inventions. An invention is defined as the initial model that meets a particular need, while innovation refers to the widespread adoption of that invention. For example, the light bulb was initially an invention, but when it became a widespread and ubiquitous feature of everyday life, it became an innovation. All of the inventions and innovations that have emerged from America have been adopted worldwide because they also meet the needs of people outside the country.

The ability of inventors to make money from their inventions depends on the protection of their intellectual property and patent rights. Societies that protect intellectual property rights and patents are more likely to foster inventiveness. In America, the concept of intellectual and industrial property rights has been in practice since the colonial era, and people have paid to purchase written ideas, designs, and concepts that have been officially registered. The commercial value of ideas, inventions, and designs has led many people to become inventors, and those who have succeeded have created industries in America.

The geographical conditions of the country have paved the way for innovation in America. As a country settled in the continent of America, the United States is the fourth largest country in the world in terms of land area, covering 9,631,418 km².[45] [46]Unlike Canada, it is located in the part of the North American continent close to the equator, which has made a large portion of the country suitable for living.

Due to its vast expanse, the country has examples of all climates found across the world. The generous climate in many regions is a significant factor that has allowed the country to rise as a world power in the agricultural sector. High production in the agricultural sector has led to high incomes, which have facilitated the introduction of high technology and mechanization in agricultural production. Although controversial, the application of genetic engineering in agriculture has made it possible to produce all kinds of fruits and vegetables in desired sizes and shapes, such as seedless watermelons.

Many of the primary raw materials are produced in the American continent. The iron reserves are among the world's largest, and the country is also very rich in petroleum resources. The abundance of iron reserves, along with other unique opportunities in America, has made it possible to create many innovations in the iron and steel industry. The abundance of petroleum resources has also provided the

---

[45] Acquisition and Retention of U.S. Citizenship and Nationality. U.S. Department of State. http://www.state.gov/documents/organization/86755.pdf. (10.07.2011).

[46] Biggest Countries, http://geography.about.com/od/countryinformation/a/bigcountries.htm, (10.07.2011).

required source for the development of petrochemical and plastic industries.[47]

The vast expanse of America's continental land has many consequences, including large-scale production and consumption. As a country of a size approaching that of the European continent (Europe has an area of 10,400,000 km^2)[48], the United States has the resources and demand to create a global industry, as stated above. Due to its large size, transportation of goods and people is a significant requirement. Inventions in transportation machines on land and in the air can be attributed to the large demand for transportation. The need for communication and financial infrastructure for trade has emerged. With telegraph and telephone communication, banking has become a fundamental requirement. The production of rails needed for the transportation infrastructure in America would be enough to lay tracks across all of Europe. Again, rail production requires steel factories that can produce rails and a sufficient amount of iron to be processed in these factories. The exceptional size of the country provides a foundation for industrial production.

In 1736, Benjamin Franklin, who would later be among the founders of America, traveled through five states and understood where they united and where they diverged.[49] Although each state had different characteristics based on its context, the most important unifying factor was the use of the same language everywhere. Speaking the same language

---

[47] Natural Resources in the US, http://geography.about.com/library/cia/blcusa.htm, (10.07.2011).

[48] Size of Europe, http://www.world-atlas.us/europe.htm, (10.07.2011).

[49] Burlingame, Roger., Benjamin Franklin, Envoy Extraordinary, Coward-McCann, New York, 1967, p. 36.

throughout a vast geography not only created a sense of nationhood, but also provided a commercial convenience.

In 18th century America, news traveled slowly because communication technology had not yet advanced significantly. It was possible to send news by ship along the coast, but when the news arrived, it was often outdated by several months. Inland, it was possible to transmit news by horseback to small towns, but this news was also delayed due to adverse weather and road conditions. Newspaper owners were the ones who cared most about the postal service. The ability to sell more newspapers depended on the ability to distribute them quickly and to a wider area.

In the 1790s, 3.9 million Americans lived along the Atlantic coast or no more than 100 miles inland. The low population in the interior of North America was due to transportation difficulties and costs. Even if people were able to establish settlements in the interior of America, mutual transportation of goods from the coastal areas to the interior was problematic.[50] In order to solve this problem, solutions that would both speed up transportation and reduce transportation costs had to be found. One solution was road construction. However, at that time, the primary means of transportation were horses and wagons. Although smooth roads could speed up transportation, it was not possible to exceed the physical speed of horses.

Another alternative for long-distance transportation at that time was river transportation. However, there was not always a connection between the cities where river transportation was desired. To make river transportation logical, canals could be opened between rivers and lakes, allowing riverboats to carry passengers and goods from river to river. The first thirty years

---

[50] Schweikart, Larry, and Lynne Doti. American Entrepreneur: A History of Business in the United States. Amacom, 2009, pg. 81-82.

of the 1800s saw both road and canal construction in America. However, canals were not initially a perfect solution for transportation. Going with the river's current was easy and fast, but going against the current was very slow. Rowing was used to try to move against the river, but this transportation effort was highly inefficient. Although higher speeds were reached going with the river's current than with land transportation, the problem of moving against the current had to be solved.

The story of America's development is a series of intertwined problem-and-solution stories. Each solution to a problem has brought about another problem, which has led to the development of a new solution. The situation in the transportation industry is no different. While river transport is a solution to transportation problems, it also brings with it the challenge of traveling against the current. Thus, every solution in America has brought about a new problem, creating a constant cycle of problem-solving. However, every problem that comes with a solution opens a window of opportunity for creativity.

One of the main debates about creativity is whether humans can be truly creative from scratch. While humans cannot physically create something out of nothing, they can come up with something new at a conceptual level. For instance, Mark Zuckerberg imagined Facebook before it existed, and the Wright brothers created plans for an airplane that did not yet exist. However, the originality of these and similar ventures can be questioned. David Kord Murray, the author of "Borrowing Brilliance,"[51] points out that all ideas are built on other ideas. He claims that there can be no completely original idea, and that it is not possible to create something new from nothing, even at a conceptual level. "Every idea is born out of other ideas. Creativity is actually something borrowed,"

---

[51] Murray, David Kord. Borrowing brilliance: the six steps to business innovation by building on the ideas of others. penguin, 2009.

Murray says. He also suggests that creativity is essentially a new combination of existing elements. He cites Albert Einstein's quote, "The secret to creativity is knowing how to hide your sources," as a reference point. Murray finds it natural that even Isaac Newton and William Shakespeare were accused of using other people's ideas. When accused of stealing ideas while creating "Calculus," Isaac Newton explained the situation by saying, "I stood on the shoulders of giants to see further." Every new idea builds on some old ideas.

The author of "Steal Like an Artist," Austin Kleon, also states that the best way to find new ideas for creativity is to find other good ideas. According to Kleon, the source of inspiration is finding new ideas that one likes. He also emphasizes, with a reference to Salvador Dali, that those who are afraid of imitating will not be able to create anything.[52]

As a community of nations immigrating to America, new ideas and inventions have been built on the knowledge inherited from the past. In other words, not only have people migrated, but knowledge has migrated from the places they came from. America's popular breakfast item, the bagel, was brought by the Jews.[53] Pizza came from Italy[54], and the sandwich from England[55].

Dave Murray points out that creative ideas emerge from a problem and its definition. The breadth of the problem

---

[52] Kleon, Austin. Steal Like an Artist 10th Anniversary Gift Edition with a New Afterword by the Author: 10 Things Nobody Told You About Being Creative. Workman Publishing, 2022.

[53] Balinska, Maria. The bagel: The surprising history of a modest bread. Yale University Press, 2008.

[54] Helstosky, Carol. Pizza: a global history. Reaktion books, 2008.

[55] Wilson, Bee. Sandwich: A global history. Reaktion Books, 2010.

definition affects the solution of the problem. To achieve the main breakthrough in solving a problem, it is necessary to borrow ideas from previously solved problems. For instance, the library card system was taken as an example for shortening passport queues at customs. Based on the model of a library member who quickly processes the transaction with a magnetic card, a model of a passenger passing through customs with a magnetic passport has been designed.

Creativity arises from the combination of two different and unrelated ideas in almost every example. According to Jonah Lehrer, the author of "Imagination,"[56] inventions always arise as a result of merging two different things. For example, in the Star Wars[57] saga, George Lucas linked medieval themes to a science fiction movie set in the late third millennium. Medieval knights became Jedi Knights, and their swords turned into lightsabers.[58]

The next stage of creativity is the incubation period. Many inventions were discovered not during research but after taking a break from it. For example, the photocopier was developed over a 15-year period in the United States. The efforts of the first inventors in creating the photocopier were left dormant until they were transferred to Xerox, where they bore fruit.[59]

---

[56] Lehrer, Jonah. Imagine: How creativity works. Houghton Mifflin Harcourt, 2012.

[57] George Lucas, dir. Star Wars: A New Hope. 1977; Beverly Hills, CA: 20th Century Fox, 2011.

[58] Markus Hearn, Ron Howard, The Cinema of George Lucas, Harry N. Abrams, 2005.

[59] Owen, David. Copies in Seconds: How a Lone Inventor and an Unknown Company Created the Biggest Communication Breakthrough Since Gutenberg--Chester Carlson and the Birth of the Xerox Machine. Simon and Schuster, 2008.

The most important stage of creativity is the evaluation stage. Where a project will end up depends on the positive, negative, and emotional evaluations made about the project. In America, people have reacted to certain technologies over time.

According to David Kord Murray, creativity in America has evolved sequentially through problem definition, borrowing ideas, merging, incubation, and evaluation processes. Even if an invention emerges at the end of this process, all these processes continue as a process of improving the existing technology. For example, the invention of the razor simplified daily shaving for men. With a new definition of shaving technology, electric razors and wet razors were invented. Single-blade razors were followed by double-blade, triple-blade, and six-blade razors.[60] In other words, every invention was followed by continuous improvements.

Creativity is the combination of two different elements to create something new, and the blending of cultural differences in particular provides ample opportunities for many new inventions to emerge. The ethnic diversity in America and the cultural backgrounds of each ethnic group have been a great asset to the country, as they have led to the emergence of new perspectives. Diversity in America has allowed for different cultural perspectives and solutions to come to the fore, leading to many innovations in fields ranging from food to fashion, technology to literature, and religion to law.

In America, diversity and multiculturalism have been important resources not only for businesses but also for the government, educational institutions, and civil society

---

[60] McKibben, Gordon. Cutting Edge: Gilette's Journey to Global Leadership, Harvard Business Review Books, 1997.

organizations.[61] However, during America's founding, diversity was more of a natural process than a managed one. Nowadays, many institutions are committed to bringing people of different ethnic and cultural backgrounds together, but they do not always know how to leverage this diversity to their advantage.[62] Nevertheless, it is widely believed that diversity is a source of creativity and innovation.[63] Eric von Hippel, the author of "Democratizing Innovation,"[64] argues that innovation requires more than just diversity - it also requires the involvement of a much larger community, including users, not just design teams.

It can be said that America's continuous renewal is largely dependent on its capacity for innovation and creativity. Prominent companies such as Apple and Google regularly introduce new innovative products every year, surpassing their past achievements and reinventing themselves. This mindset sets America apart from other nations, making it unbeatable or invincible.

3.1.2.1 Criticism to American Creativity and Innovation

Creativity and innovation are crucial elements of American entrepreneurship and have played a significant role in the country's economic and social development. However, while creativity and innovation can drive progress, they have also been disruptive forces in various aspects of society. For example, technological advancements have replaced jobs and

---

[61] Thomas, Roosevelt., Building on the Premise of Diversity, Amacom, 2005.

[62] Johnson, Michelle T., The Diversity Code: Unlock the Secrets to Making Differences Work in the Real World, Amacom, 2010.

[63] Kennedy, Debbie, Putting Our Differences to Work: The Fastest Way to Innovation, Leadership, and High Performance, Berret Koehler Business, 2008.

[64] Hippel, Eric Von, **Democratizing Innovation,** MIT Press, 2006.

industries, leaving some communities struggling to adapt. The rise of digital media has challenged traditional business models, particularly in the publishing and music industries.

Innovation can be disruptive to social order. The introduction of new technologies, particularly in the digital space, has the potential to change social dynamics and norms. For example, the proliferation of social media platforms has changed the way people communicate and consume information, leading to concerns about the impact on mental health[65] and political polarization.[66] The increasing use of automation and artificial intelligence in industries like manufacturing and transportation also raises concerns about job displacement and income inequality.[67]

Creativity and innovation can also have negative impacts on the environment and natural resources. New technologies and industries can lead to increased resource consumption and pollution, which can have long-term consequences for the planet.[68] It is essential to balance economic growth with environmental sustainability to ensure that the benefits of innovation are not outweighed by its negative impacts.[69]

---

[65] Bashir, Hilal, and Shabir Ahmad Bhat. "Effects of social media on mental health: A review." International Journal of Indian Psychology 4.3 (2017): 125-131.

[66] Kubin, Emily, and Christian von Sikorski. "The role of (social) media in political polarization: a systematic review." Annals of the International Communication Association 45.3 (2021): 188-206.

[67] McClure, Paul K. ""You're fired," says the robot: The rise of automation in the workplace, technophobes, and fears of unemployment." Social Science Computer Review 36.2 (2018): 139-156.

[68] Chen, Yang, Liang Cheng, and Chien-Chiang Lee. "How does the use of industrial robots affect the ecological footprint? International evidence." Ecological Economics 198 (2022): 107483.

[69] Costa, Carlos M., et al. "Recycling and environmental issues of lithium-ion batteries: Advances, challenges and opportunities." Energy Storage Materials 37 (2021): 433-465.

A classic example of this balance is the oil industry. The discovery and extraction of oil have brought tremendous economic benefits to the United States, but they have also had significant environmental consequences. Climate change, oil spills,[70] and other environmental disasters have highlighted the need to find more sustainable energy sources and reduce our reliance on fossil fuels.

Despite these challenges, innovation and creativity remained key drivers of the American economy. Many successful entrepreneurs have embraced sustainable and socially responsible practices, recognizing the importance of balancing economic growth with environmental and social responsibility. For example, Patagonia, a popular outdoor clothing company, has championed environmental causes and sustainability, while also growing into a profitable business.[71]

In conclusion, while innovation and creativity have been disruptive forces in the economy, social order, and the environment, they have also been essential to American entrepreneurship. It is important to continue to foster and encourage innovative ideas while also considering the potential consequences and taking steps to mitigate any negative impacts.

3.1.2.2. Innovation and Creativity in Europe

The assertion that the United States is the foremost nation in creativity and innovation should be approached with caution, as it is essential to recognize that these qualities are not

---

[70] Kingston, Paul F. "Long-term environmental impact of oil spills." Spill Science & Technology Bulletin 7.1-2 (2002): 53-61.

[71] Michel, Gwendolyn M., et al. "Stories we wear: Promoting sustainability practices with the case of Patagonia." Family and Consumer Sciences Research Journal 48.2 (2019): 165-180.

limited to any specific country or region. While the US has produced many influential inventors, entrepreneurs, and businessmen, it is crucial to consider the historical, social, and economic elements that have contributed to the growth of creativity and innovation in the United States, and to compare them with those present in Europe.

Europe has a long and illustrious history of producing significant innovations and creative works,[72] including the printing press, steam engine, and the works of Shakespeare, Beethoven, and Picasso. Nevertheless, the pace of innovation in Europe may have been slower than that in the US due to several factors, including a more entrenched social hierarchy, a less favorable legal and economic climate for entrepreneurs, and a more conservative cultural atmosphere.[73]

This study highlights that the US culture of entrepreneurship is one of the critical elements contributing to the development of creativity and innovation. The United States values individual initiative and risk-taking, encouraging many people to pursue their business ideas. The country's legal and economic systems provide a favorable environment for entrepreneurship, with strong protections for intellectual property and relatively low barriers to entry for new businesses. Conversely, European countries have more intricate regulatory frameworks and higher tax rates than the US, which can make it more challenging for new businesses to establish themselves.

Another significant factor contributing to the development of creativity and innovation in the United States is the country's

---

[72] Crouzet, François. A History of the European Economy, 1000-2000: 1000-2000. University of Virginia Press, 2001.

[73] Persson, Karl Gunnar, and Paul Sharp. An economic history of Europe. Cambridge University Press, 2015.

relative youth. While Europe has a rich cultural and intellectual history that spans thousands of years, the United States is a relatively new country shaped by waves of immigration and rapid technological advancement.[74] This has fostered a sense of dynamism and forward momentum, driving innovation in various fields.

In conclusion, while the United States has undoubtedly been at the forefront of creativity and innovation over the past few centuries, it is critical to acknowledge that these qualities are not exclusive to any particular nation or region. Instead, creativity and innovation are complex phenomena influenced by a wide range of historical, social, and economic factors. These factors helped the US to be an open field for creativity and innovation.

---

[74] Hart, David M., and Zoltan J. Acs. "High-tech immigrant entrepreneurship in the United States." Economic Development Quarterly 25.2 (2011): 116-129.n

Only those who will risk going too far can possibly find out how far one can go.
T. S. Eliot

3.1.3. Risk Taking

Entrepreneurship and innovation have been the driving forces behind the economic success of the United States. The country has been able to create a culture of innovation and entrepreneurship that has allowed for the creation of new businesses, industries, and technologies. One of the key factors contributing to the success of entrepreneurship and innovation in the US has been the country's risk-taking culture.

In his book "Against the Gods," Peter Bernstein articulates that taking risks essentially means leveraging the future for the benefit of the present. Those who have mastered the art of risk-taking have succeeded in transforming the future from a looming threat into a promising opportunity. Advancements in technology, economic expansion, and elevations in quality of life have all materialized as direct outcomes of embracing risk. Consequently, the progress of a nation is intrinsically tied to the risk-taking capabilities of its populace.[75]

The history of entrepreneurship in the US dates back to the country's founding, where the concept of taking risks was embedded in the culture of the time. The colonists who settled in America were risk-takers, leaving behind their familiar surroundings to start a new life in an unknown land. This spirit of adventure and risk-taking became part of the American identity, and was a driving force behind the country's rapid expansion in the 19th century.

Taking risks has been one of the most important characteristics of the American character. In the beginning, European immigrants took a great risk by setting out to establish their lives on an unknown continent. Once they

---

[75] Bernstein, Peter L., and Peter L. Bernstein. Against the gods: The remarkable story of risk. New York: Wiley, 1996.

reached America, moving west into the unknown required continuous risk-taking, despite the natural hazards and risks posed by Native Americans. However, they continued to advance. When they reached all the unreachable geographical points in the country, the field of risk-taking expanded from geographical advancement to science, art, and business. Creativity, especially when combined with risk-taking, has led to many innovations. For example, the Wright Brothers risked their lives and livelihoods while trying to invent an airplane. Their creative approach, combined with their own risk-taking in testing their design experiments, led to a groundbreaking invention that revolutionized world transportation.

The concept of entrepreneurship in the US has always been closely linked to risk-taking. Entrepreneurs are individuals who take calculated risks to start and grow a business. They are willing to invest their time, money, and energy into an idea that may or may not succeed. This mindset has been a driving force behind the creation of new industries and technologies in the US. To create change, one must give up the security and comfort of what already exists. One cannot establish a new business while continuing to work professionally and receive a salary. To establish a new business, one must take risks, resign and take action to establish a new business. The creators of Hotmail, Indian-American Sabeer Bhatia and Jack Smith, resigned from their professional jobs to establish Hotmail, a web-based email system.[76] Jeff Bezos took the risk of starting an online book-selling business using a new technology called the internet,

---

[76] Po Bronson, "HotMale: Sabeer Bhatia started his company on USD 300.000 and sold it two years later for USD 400 million. So is he lucky or great?, Wired, Issue, 6.12 December 1998.

which was completely based on bookstores for sales at the time.[77]

One of the defining characteristics of the US entrepreneurial culture is the acceptance of failure. In the US, failure is seen as a learning experience, and an opportunity to try again. This culture of embracing failure has created an environment where entrepreneurs are willing to take risks and experiment with new ideas.

The risk-taking culture in the US has also had a significant impact on innovation. Innovation is the process of creating something new that adds value to society. It requires creativity and risk-taking, both of which are encouraged in the US entrepreneurial culture. This culture has led to the creation of new technologies, products, and services that have transformed the way we live and work.

The risk-taking culture in the US has been a major driver of economic growth. Entrepreneurs create new businesses, which in turn create jobs and generate wealth. This has led to the creation of new industries and the growth of existing ones, contributing to the overall economic success of the country.

While the risk-taking culture in the US has been a major driver of entrepreneurship and innovation, it is not without its challenges. The current regulatory environment can make it difficult for entrepreneurs to start and grow a business. Access to funding can also be a challenge, particularly for those who do not have established networks or connections.

The US risk-taking culture has been a defining characteristic of the country's entrepreneurial and innovative spirit. It has allowed for the creation of new businesses, industries, and

---

[77] Brad, Stone, The Everything Store: Jeff Bezos and the Age of Amazon, Little, Brown and Company, 2013.

technologies that have transformed the world. However, the challenges facing entrepreneurs today suggest that more needs to be done to support the next generation of risk-takers and innovators. With the right support, the US risk-taking culture can continue to drive entrepreneurship and innovation for years to come.

The level of risk taking is a determining factor of a society's entrepreneurship level. In a country like Turkey where civil service is highly valued, risk taking and entrepreneurship based on risk are at lower levels. In the United States, however, risk taking can be considered a cultural identity element.

Peter Bernstein, in his book "Against the Gods," defines risk taking as offering the future as a service to today. Those who manage to take risks have been able to turn the future from a threat into an opportunity. Technological development, economic growth, and increased quality of life have all emerged as a result of risk taking. Therefore, a country's development is largely dependent on its members' ability to take risks.

Risk taking, in a sense, means creating options. Because while risk-free options are available to everyone, those who choose to take risks have created and chosen an unseen option. The revelation and implementation of this unseen option enable social, economic, or technological developments. Trying to build a train while horse and carriage were still a primary means of transportation, is taking a risk by investing in it. However, with the invention of the train, a new transportation option was presented to society.

According to John Kadvany and Baruch Fishoff, the level of risk taking is related to a society's self-identification.[78] The way a society deals with uncertainties about itself and the world, resistance to risk, and intellectual response demonstrate a society's nature. As stated in the introduction, in societies with low risk-taking levels, there is more demand for government bureaucracies, while in societies with high risk-taking levels, there is demand for more entrepreneurship and liberty.

To take chances, it's important to let go a little and go with the flow. If everything is too controlled, it's hard to discover anything new or go beyond what is already known. According to Lehrer, if musicians always avoid playing the wrong note or if people constantly avoid making mistakes, they will lose the opportunity to discover something new. In fact, every mistake made by taking risks opens a new door in the world of creativity and imagination.

In his book "Little Bets," Peter Sims notes that the most successful entrepreneurs did not set out with big ideas, but rather discovered them over time.[79] David Galenson believes there are two types of innovators in the world: conceptual innovators and experimental innovators. Conceptual innovators like Mozart seek big ideas from a young age and make great innovations at a young age. Experimental innovators, on the other hand, create big innovations through trial and error.[80] They persistently and steadfastly keep trying and are not afraid of failure. They are not afraid to be left behind as a result of their mistakes and failures.

---

[78] John Kadvany,Baruch Fishoff, Risk: A Brief Introduction, OUP Oxford, 2011.

[79] Peter Sims, Little Bets, How Breakthrough Ideas Emerge from Small Discoveries, Simon Schuster, 2013.

[80] David Galenson, Old Masters and Young Geniuses, Princeton, 2005.

The greatest benefit of working in this way is seen particularly in situations where everything is uncertain. Those who can act against the threat of failure caused by uncertainty can make progress. Thomas Edison's famous quote confirms this: "I have not failed. I've just found 10,000 ways that won't work."

According to Peter Sims, author of "Little Bets," entrepreneurs take calculated risks rather than reckless risks. Rather than focusing on what they will gain from the general idea, they focus on what they will lose. For the Wright Brothers, trying to build an airplane, it was more important not to lose their lives than to fly. While those who attempted to build airplanes personally tested and crashed their planes, the Wright Brothers built a model of their planned airplane and tested it in a wind tunnel to see if it worked. This way, they did not risk their lives while they were able to determine if their models would work. Jeff Bezos used his garage to start his book-selling business after leaving his job in New York. Thus, he risked only the time he would spend and the inconvenience of having to work from his home. Similarly, Henry Ford built his first car in a shed in front of his house. Facebook founder Mark Zuckerberg worked on software development for a long time with a budget of less than $50,000.[81]

Risk-taking is a learnable skill. Those who struggle with taking risks often lack the ability to develop their risk-taking capabilities because they generally avoid taking risks. However, those who constantly take risks also develop their risk-taking abilities with each risk they take. Taking action and making mistakes as soon as possible provide an opportunity to discover these mistakes and learn how to do things right. Experimentation or trial and error is not just an activity done only in laboratories. Moving to another city,

---

[81] Galloway, Scott. The four: the hidden DNA of Amazon, Apple, Facebook, and Google. Penguin, 2018.

starting a business, launching a product, or adding something new to a product can all be considered experiments or trials.

Every trial does not only mean taking risks but also means learning by doing. In this sense, every trial carries the meaning of taking risks, learning, and developing oneself. In America, since many trials are done publicly, one person's experiment inspires courage and teaches other members of society who follow their trials.

Hobbies and personal curiosity also play an important role in the culture of risk-taking. Thomas Edison approached learning the mechanics and principles of the telegraph machine as a hobby. As a result of his experimental nature, he was able to transmit two messages simultaneously over a single wire.[82]

Entrepreneurs have taken risks by dedicating themselves to their areas of interest. Ray Kroc operated a McDonald's restaurant before buying the entire company from the McDonald brothers by taking on a large debt once he had mastered the business.[83]

An important element in taking risks for innovation is to redefine the definition. Google's founders discovered that what they had developed for an effective library search engine was actually a general search engine.[84]

---

[82] Laurie Carlson, Thomas Edison: His Life and Ideas, Chicago Review Press, 2006, pg. 116.

[83] Ray Kroc ve Robert Anderson, Grinding It Out: The Making Of McDonald's, Saint Martin's Paperbacks, Saint Martin, 1992.

[84] Vise, David A., and Mark Malseed. "The Google story: Inside the hottest business, media, and technology success of our time, paperback edition." New York: Delta Trade (2006).

When innovating, it is also important to rethink and redesign the risk and business model. For example, Ray Kroc, who opened the first McDonald's restaurant, foresaw that McDonald's could become a chain across the country and even the world. Although it was not clear whether this was possible at first, he took the risk and expanded his business by redesigning it.

For an experiment to turn into a discovery, and a discovery into an invention, there is a need for continuous improvement, data collection, and gathering people's thoughts. Companies like Microsoft and Google in America release beta versions of new products and gather feedback from people to make improvements based on that feedback. They continue to receive feedback from users after the product is released, turning experiments into successful endeavors instead of risks.

3.1.3.1 Criticism to Risk Taking

American entrepreneurship has long been associated with a willingness to take risks. This trait has been a key driver of innovation and progress in the American economy, but it has also had its downsides. Understanding the critical perspectives on risk taking is important for assessing the role of entrepreneurship in shaping the economy, society, and the environment.

One perspective is that risk taking can be disruptive to the economy. Entrepreneurial ventures are inherently risky, and many fail. When entrepreneurs invest in new ideas and businesses, they are taking a gamble that their efforts will be rewarded with success. However, when these ventures fail, they can have a negative impact on the economy, causing investors to lose money and disrupting the market.[85] In addition, the focus on risk taking can lead to a culture of short-term gains, where companies prioritize immediate profits over long-term sustainability.

Another perspective is that risk taking can be disruptive to social order. Entrepreneurs often challenge established norms and disrupt traditional ways of doing things.[86] While this can lead to innovation and progress, it can also create tension and conflict in society. For example, the rise of the sharing economy has disrupted traditional industries such as transportation and hospitality, leading to debates over issues such as worker rights and consumer safety. In addition, risk taking can exacerbate existing inequalities, as those with the resources to take risks are often those who benefit the most from the rewards of entrepreneurship.

In recent years, the blockchain and cryptocurrency industries have been a prime example of the critical role of risk-taking in entrepreneurship.[87] These industries have been disruptive in many ways, challenging traditional models of finance and creating new opportunities for innovation.

One example of risk-taking in the blockchain industry is the creation of decentralized finance (DeFi) protocols. These protocols allow users to access financial services without

---

[85] Eggers, J. P., and Lin Song. "Dealing with failure: Serial entrepreneurs and the costs of changing industries between ventures." Academy of Management Journal 58.6 (2015): 1785-1803.

[86] McGregor, Moira, Barry Brown, and Mareike Glöss. "Disrupting the cab: Uber, ridesharing and the taxi industry." Journal of Peer Production 6 (2015).

[87] Binford, Jason B. "The Role of Federal and State Regulators in Crypto Bankruptcies." American Bankruptcy Institute Journal 42.5 (2023): 28-48.

relying on traditional financial institutions.[88] While this concept has the potential to revolutionize the financial industry, it also poses risks such as security vulnerabilities and lack of regulation.

Another example is the creation of non-fungible tokens (NFTs), which are unique digital assets that can be bought and sold on blockchain networks.[89] NFTs have opened up new possibilities for creators to monetize their work, but also pose risks such as high volatility in the market and potential legal issues around ownership and copyright.

In the cryptocurrency industry, the creation of new digital currencies is a prime example of risk-taking. While Bitcoin was the first and remains the most well-known cryptocurrency, there are now thousands of other cryptocurrencies in existence, each with their own unique features and potential use cases. However, the lack of regulation and the high volatility of cryptocurrency markets have made investing in these currencies a risky proposition.[90]

The blockchain and cryptocurrency industries have been disruptive and innovative precisely because of the risks taken by their entrepreneurs. While these risks have the potential to create significant disruption in the economy and other sectors, they also have the potential to create new opportunities and push boundaries in ways that were previously unimaginable.

---

[88] Xu, Teng Andrea, and Jiahua Xu. "A short survey on business models of decentralized finance (DeFi) protocols." arXiv preprint arXiv:2202.07742 (2022).

[89] Fortnow, Matt, and QuHarrison Terry. The NFT Handbook: How to create, sell and buy non-fungible tokens. John Wiley & Sons, 2021.

[90] Xie, Rain. "Why China had to ban cryptocurrency but the US did not: a comparative analysis of regulations on crypto-markets between the US and China." Wash. U. Global Stud. L. Rev. 18 (2019): 457.

3.1.3.2. Concept of Risk Taking in Europe

The lack of a risk-taking culture in continental Europe between the 17th and 20th centuries is a complex issue that can be attributed to a combination of historical, social, and economic factors. One of the key factors is the capital accumulation and control by the noble classes of Europe, who were more focused on maintaining their social and economic status than taking risks in entrepreneurial ventures. Another factor was the labor structure, which included serfs and other lower classes who did not have the means or opportunity to take risks. Additionally, those who did have the means and willingness to take risks often emigrated to the Americas, leaving behind a more risk-averse population in Europe. In this part, these factors will be explored in more detail..

The first reason why Europe did not have a similar culture of risk-taking to that of the US between 1600 and now is the way capital accumulation and control were concentrated in the hands of the nobility and other privileged classes. In Europe, the landed nobility often controlled vast estates and accumulated wealth through rent-seeking activities rather than through entrepreneurial ventures.[91] This left little opportunity for individuals outside of the aristocracy to accumulate capital and take risks with new business ideas.

For example, during the Industrial Revolution in Britain, the vast majority of capital for new factories and businesses came from the landed gentry, who had accumulated wealth through their control of agricultural land.[92] This made it difficult for working-class entrepreneurs to access capital and take risks,

---

[91] Dewald, Jonathan. *The European Nobility, 1400-1800.* Vol. 9. Cambridge University Press, 1996, pg. 12-14.

[92] Allen, Robert. "Capital accumulation, technological change, and the distribution of income during the British Industrial Revolution." (2005).

---

as they were often shut out of the financial networks controlled by the aristocracy.

Another factor that limited risk-taking in Europe was the labor structure. In many European countries, feudalism[93] persisted long after it had disappeared in the US, with serfs bound to the land and subject to the whims of the local lord. This made it difficult for individuals to break free from the constraints of their social class and pursue entrepreneurial ventures. The rigid social hierarchy also made it difficult for individuals to form networks and collaborate on new business ideas.

For example, in Russia, serfdom was only abolished in 1861, and even after that, the peasantry remained tied to the land and subject to the control of the nobility. This made it difficult for individuals to pursue entrepreneurial ventures or accumulate capital.

Additionally, many of the risk-takers in Europe during this time period emigrated to the US. For example, during the 19th and early 20th centuries, millions of Europeans emigrated to the US in search of better economic opportunities. Many of these individuals were risk-takers who were willing to leave behind their homes and families to pursue a better life in a new country. This left behind a population in Europe that was less inclined to take risks and pursue entrepreneurial ventures.

Finally, capital control was also a factor that limited risk-taking in Europe. In many European countries, the monarch had control over the economy, and this often led to restrictions on trade and investment. This made it difficult for

---

[93] Brenner, Robert. "Feudalism." *Marxian Economics*. London: Palgrave Macmillan UK, 1990. 170-185.

individuals to take risks and pursue new business ideas, as they were often subject to strict government control.

For example, in France, Louis XIV's mercantilist policies[94] limited trade and investment and made it difficult for individuals to pursue new business ventures. This led to a culture of risk-aversion and conservatism that persisted for centuries.

In summary, the combination of capital accumulation and control in the hands of the privileged classes, the persistence of feudalism and rigid social hierarchies, emigration of risk-takers to the US, and capital control by monarchs all contributed to a lack of risk-taking culture in Europe between 1600 and now. These factors made it difficult for individuals to accumulate capital, take risks, and pursue entrepreneurial ventures.

---

[94] Peukert, Helge. "Mercantilism." *Handbook of the History of Economic Thought: Insights on the Founders of Modern Economics*. New York, NY: Springer New York, 2011. 93-121.

Competition has been shown to be useful up to a certain point and no further, but cooperation, which is the thing we must strive for today, begins where competition leaves off.
Franklin D. Roosevelt

3.1.4. Competition and Renewal

Competition in the US has been a driving force behind the growth of entrepreneurship and innovation. The US has a long history of market competition, which has encouraged entrepreneurs to create new and innovative products and services to meet the needs of consumers. From the early days of the country, entrepreneurs were able to compete with each other in a relatively open market, which gave them the opportunity to innovate and differentiate themselves from their competitors.[95]

One of the most notable examples of this competition can be seen in the growth of the automobile industry in the early 20th century.[96] The US was home to a number of automobile manufacturers, including Ford,[97] General Motors, and Chrysler, which competed fiercely with each other to produce the best cars at the lowest prices. This competition led to a number of innovations in the industry, including the introduction of the assembly line, which revolutionized manufacturing and allowed for the mass production of cars at a lower cost.

Renewal has also been a key factor in the growth of entrepreneurship and innovation[98] in the US. The country has a culture of constantly questioning the status quo and seeking new and better ways of doing things. This has encouraged

---

[95] Schumpeter, Joseph A. "Entrepreneurship as innovation." *University of Illinois at Urbana-Champaign's Academy for Entrepreneurial Leadership Historical Research Reference in Entrepreneurship* (2000).

[96] Esch, Elizabeth. *The color line and the assembly line: Managing race in the Ford empire.* Vol. 50. Univ of California Press, 2018.

[97] Holweg, Matthias. "The evolution of competition in the automotive industry." *Build to order: The road to the 5-day car.* London: Springer London, 2008. 13-34.

[98] Birkinshaw, Julian. "Entrepreneurship in the global firm: Enterprise and renewal." *Entrepreneurship in the Global Firm* (2000): 1-168.

—

entrepreneurs to challenge traditional ways of thinking and to develop innovative products and services that disrupt existing markets.

One of the most notable examples of this renewal can be seen in the growth of the tech industry in the US in the late 20th and early 21st centuries. Companies like Apple, Microsoft, and Google have revolutionized the way we interact with technology[99], and have challenged traditional business models in industries like music, publishing, and advertising. These companies have been able to do this because of their willingness to challenge conventional thinking and to develop new and innovative approaches to solving problems.

Competition and renewal have also been supported by a number of other factors in the US. For example, the country's legal and regulatory framework has generally been supportive of entrepreneurship and innovation, with strong protections for intellectual property and relatively low barriers to entry for new businesses.[100] In addition, the US has a strong education system that has produced a skilled workforce that is able to innovate and compete in a rapidly changing global economy.

The desire to win and achieve, which is identified with the concept of the American Dream, drives entrepreneurs to develop their projects faster, better, and at a lower cost than their competitors. The constant pursuit of improvement in a competitive environment leads to improvements in various performance parameters in all areas, and sometimes even to

---

[99] Galloway, Scott. *The four: the hidden DNA of Amazon, Apple, Facebook, and Google*. Penguin, 2018.

[100] Sobel, Russell. "Regulation and Entrepreneurship: Theory, Impacts, and Implications." *The Center for Growth and Opportunity* (2023).

revolutions or disruptive innovations.[101] For example, music albums progressed from vinyl to cassette, from cassette to CD, and from CD to MP3.[102] However, each media went through many improvements in itself. Vinyl records were replaced by plastic records, which were of better quality. Then, tapes appeared as a radical advancement. Tapes, which constantly improved in terms of magnetic recording quality, were replaced by CDs. Audio files, which took up a lot of space, were replaced by MP3 files with improvements. Finally, there was another radical revolution, and music tracks were sold for the first time on Apple's iTunes, an online music supermarket in America. This story of the decades-long presentation of music albums to users has become a history of continuous improvement and renewal through competition and technological development.

Entrepreneurs in America constantly strive for improvement both within their own businesses and in competition with the world. Competition in America is not only among businesses and organizations, but also among individuals. In the business world, constant self-improvement, gaining more education, and acquiring skills are necessary to find employment. Similarly, the entire education system is established to attract the most successful students.[103] However, since students have the right to choose their schools and universities, these institutions are in constant competition to be more successful than others.

---

[101] Christensen, Clay, Michael E. Raynor, and Rory McDonald. *Disruptive innovation.* Brighton, MA, USA: Harvard Business Review, 2013.

[102] Noll, A. Michael. *The evolution of media.* Rowman & Littlefield, 2007.

[103] Davies, Scott, and Floyd M. Hammack. "The channeling of student competition in higher education: Comparing Canada and the US." *The Journal of Higher Education* 76.1 (2005): 89-106.

Exams such as SAT, GMAT, and GRE constantly put all students in a competitive environment.[104] This competition provides an opportunity for each student to be academically more successful. Since these exams do not rank students but only provide a score, there may be ten thousand students who have achieved a perfect score on a particular exam. When applying to a specific school, these students try to prove their superiority in areas such as art, sports, or science projects when they are academically equal to students applying to Harvard, for example.[105] In America, not ranking students academically and providing equal opportunities has resulted in competition first for academic success, then for non-academic areas and development.

Hospitals, non-governmental organizations, students, athletes, cities, and states are also in a race and competition in America. This race and competition lead to improvements or revolutionary innovations in every area.

In conclusion, competition and renewal have been essential to the growth of entrepreneurship and innovation in the US. The country's culture of competition and its willingness to challenge the status quo have encouraged entrepreneurs to develop new and innovative products and services that have transformed industries and improved people's lives. While there have been challenges along the way, the US has generally been successful in fostering an environment that supports competition and renewal, and this has contributed to its success as a global leader in entrepreneurship and innovation.

---

[104] McManus, James. "An essay review of: THE TESTING TRAP by Andrew J. Strenio, Jr." *The Review of Higher Education* 5.1 (1981): 49.

[105] Synnott, Marcia. *The half-opened door: Discrimination and admissions at Harvard, Yale, and Princeton, 1900-1970.* Routledge, 2017.

Universally competition is a phenomenon that has the power to shape all areas it enters, such as biology, ecology, economics, politics, sports, and art. As a definition, competition involves the efforts of at least two competitors to surpass each other to achieve a certain goal. The main reason for competition is the unwillingness to share the reward that will be achieved after beating the rival.

In the world, animals compete for food sources. Animals and humans compete to acquire the opposite sex. The biggest characteristic of market economies is the effort of each firm to present a better product or service than their competitors to surpass them.

The phenomenon of competition has also found its counterpart in the field of biology. Charles Darwin's theory of Natural Selection is based on the idea that the species that best adapt to the environmental conditions will survive.[106] Therefore, living beings are also in competition to survive and sustain their species. The ability of living species to sustain themselves is dependent on the development of characteristics that are suitable for their environment. Chickens walk on land with three-toed feet, while ducks can swim thanks to the membranes that develop between their three-toed feet.

In market economies, competition is the effort of a company to surpass another company or companies for a certain target customer base. This phenomenon of competition allows for the provision of higher quality products and services under better conditions due to the customer's freedom of choice.

---

[106] Levine, George. *Darwin loves you: natural selection and the re-enchantment of the world*. Princeton University Press, 2008.

There is a significant difference between improvements and revolutionary innovations.[107] While improvements describe a conventional improvement in the same product or service, revolutionary innovations involve abandoning a product or service used to meet a specific need and introducing a completely new solution. Making a locomotive faster than one's competitor is an example of an improvement. Making a train car with more comfortable seats is also an example of improvement. In a world with trains and cars, inventing an airplane is a revolutionary innovation.

Competition in America leads to improvements and then to innovations. In both cases, the system in America is constantly renewing itself. Thanks to the federal state system in America, there are different laws and tax systems in each state.[108] States that offer more attractive conditions for institutions and individuals receive more migration and investment than rival states.

The concept of competition, deeply rooted in every aspect of American society, from sports to arts, from academic life to business, and from politics to religion, provides an opportunity for innovations to emerge. The impact of competition in America has gone beyond Darwin's proposition that "survival of the fittest."[109] In America, competition is not only about adapting to change, but also about creating change. Companies like Google not only adapted to changing technology, but also developed new

---

[107] Imai, Masaaki. *Kaizen*. Vol. 201. New York: Random House Business Division, 1986.

[108] Chirinko, Robert S., and Daniel J. Wilson. "Tax competition among US states: Racing to the bottom or riding on a seesaw?." *Journal of Public Economics* 155 (2017): 147-163.

[109] Balady, Gary J. "Survival of the fittest—more evidence." *New England Journal of Medicine* 346.11 (2002): 852-854.

technologies themselves. They overtook competitors and shaped the world with the innovations they offered.

3.1.4.1 Criticism to American Competition and Renewal

While American competition and renewal have been lauded for driving innovation and progress in the entrepreneurship field, they also have their fair share of criticisms. One major criticism is that competition can lead to cutthroat tactics, unethical behavior, and a focus on short-term gains over long-term sustainability.

For example, in the late 19th century, John D. Rockefeller's Standard Oil Company used aggressive tactics such as price-cutting,[110] secret rebates, and the formation of trusts to drive competitors out of business and gain a monopoly in the oil industry. While this led to short-term gains for Standard Oil, it ultimately stifled competition and innovation in the industry.

Another criticism of American competition is that it can lead to a winner-takes-all mentality[111] and widen the gap between the wealthy and the rest of society. This can lead to a lack of access to resources for those who are unable to compete at the same level.

In the tech industry, competition has led to a focus on constant innovation and the release of new products and features at a rapid pace. While this has led to some groundbreaking advancements, it has also created a culture of "move fast and

---

[110] McGee, John S. "Predatory price cutting: the Standard Oil (NJ) case." *The Journal of Law and Economics* 1 (1958): 137-169.

[111] Evens, Tom, et al. *Winner Takes All*. Springer International Publishing, 2018.

break things,"[112] where companies prioritize speed and growth over ethical considerations and the long-term impact on society and the environment.

For example, Facebook's aggressive push for growth and data collection has been criticized for compromising user privacy and facilitating the spread of misinformation and hate speech on its platform.

Renewal, on the other hand, can also have its downsides. While it can lead to the replacement of outdated technologies and business practices with more efficient and sustainable ones, it can also lead to job loss[113] and disruption of established industries.

For instance, the rise of e-commerce has led to the closure of many brick-and-mortar stores and the loss of jobs in the retail industry.[114] While e-commerce has also created new job opportunities, the transition can be difficult for those who are unable to adapt to the new technological landscape.

In conclusion, while American competition and renewal have undoubtedly driven progress and innovation in entrepreneurship and the tech industry, they also have their fair share of criticisms. It is important for entrepreneurs and companies to consider the long-term impact of their actions on society, the environment, and individual well-being, and strive for sustainable growth and progress.

---

[112] Vardi, Moshe Y. "Move fast and break things." *Communications of the ACM* 61.9 (2018): 7-7.

[113] Nica, Elvira. "Will robots take the jobs of human workers? Disruptive technologies that may bring about jobless growth and enduring mass unemployment." *Psychosociological Issues in Human Resource Management* 6.2 (2018): 56-61.

[114] Curley, Martin, et al. "Digital disruption." *Open Innovation 2.0: The New Mode of Digital Innovation for Prosperity and Sustainability* (2018): 15-25.

3.1.4.2. Competition and Renewal in Europe

Europe, like the US, has a long history of innovation and entrepreneurship. However, the level of competition and renewal seen in the US has not been matched in continental Europe. One factor that contributed to this difference is the historical economic and political structures in Europe, which limited competition and innovation. For example, the mercantilist economic policies[115] of European nations during the 17th and 18th centuries were characterized by government intervention, trade barriers, and monopolies. These policies aimed to protect domestic industries and increase the wealth of the ruling classes, but they also limited competition and innovation.

Additionally, Europe's feudal system[116] and aristocratic society meant that wealth and power were concentrated in the hands of a small noble class, who were often resistant to change and innovation. In contrast, the US had a more open and egalitarian society, with a strong tradition of individualism and entrepreneurship. This allowed for a greater level of competition and renewal, as people were free to pursue their own ideas and businesses without facing the same obstacles as in Europe.

Furthermore, the large waves of immigration[117] to the US in the late 19th and early 20th centuries brought people from diverse backgrounds with new ideas and perspectives, which further fueled innovation and competition. In contrast,

---

[115] Wallerstein, Immanuel. *The modern world-system II: Mercantilism and the consolidation of the European world-economy, 1600–1750.* Vol. 2. Univ of California Press, 2011.

[116] Bonney, Richard. *Economic systems and state finance: The origins of the modern state in Europe 13th to 18th centuries.* Oxford University Press, 1995.

[117] Hatton, Timothy J., and Jeffrey G. Williamson. "What drove the mass migrations from Europe in the late nineteenth century?." (1992).

continental Europe was more homogenous and less welcoming to immigrants, which may have limited the diversity of ideas and stifled innovation.

Finally, Europe's political and economic landscape was marked by a number of conflicts and upheavals, such as wars, revolutions, and economic crises, that often disrupted the continuity of business activities and stifled entrepreneurship and innovation. In contrast, the United States enjoyed a relatively stable political and economic environment that provided a conducive atmosphere for the growth of businesses and innovation. The devastation of World War II left Europe with a long period of reconstruction and recovery,[118] which may have diverted resources and attention away from innovation and competition. Meanwhile, the US emerged from the war as a global superpower, with a strong economy and a focus on technological development and innovation.

Overall, while Europe has a rich history of innovation and entrepreneurship, the level of competition and renewal seen in the US has not been matched on the continent. Factors such as historical economic and political structures, social hierarchies, and immigration patterns have all contributed to this difference.

---

[118] Silverman, Dan P. *Reconstructing Europe after the Great War*. Harvard University Press, 1982.

If there is no struggle, there is no progress.
Frederick Douglass

3.1.5. Self-Made Man: The Concept of the Self-Made Individual

One of the most defining concepts of American society and mentality is the idea of the self-made individual. The idea of the self-made man,[119] or the notion that an individual can achieve success through hard work, determination, and ingenuity, has played a significant role in the history of innovation and entrepreneurship in the United States. This concept has been deeply ingrained in American culture since the country's founding, and it has inspired countless individuals to pursue their own business ideas and to strive for success.

The term "self-made man" was first coined by Frederick Douglass in a speech he gave in 1859.[120] According to Douglass, self-made individuals are those who have achieved knowledge, power, and resources on their own, and have learned to make the world livable for themselves, while also building a character. They are people who owe nothing to their birthplace, relationships, inherited wealth, or education.

Douglass believed that self-made individuals often face more obstacles than support from society. They are people who have had to acquire their education outside the traditional schools, academies, and colleges, often in unfavorable conditions, and have had to find a way to success against all odds. They are people who have grown up poor, in big, heartless cities, often without family or friends, and have had to make their own way in life.

Self-made individuals can be found in all walks of life - a university professor, a farmer, or anyone from any ethnic

---

[119] Vincent, Norah. *Self-made man*. London: Atlantic Books, 2006.

[120] Douglass, Frederick. *Self-made men*. CreateSpace Independent Publishing Platform, 2015.

background, whether white, Native American, Anglo-Saxon, or African American. Regardless of their roots or professions, they have achieved great things that have contributed to humanity. Their successes have mainly been about providing previously unavailable opportunities for others.

Douglass did not believe in the "good luck theory" that attributes success to chance or a friendly environment.[121] He believed that opportunities were important, but that effort was mandatory. For Douglass, the self-made individual is created through physical and mental effort, not luck. He saw hard work as the necessary means to achieving success.

People are like arrows in a quiver, all equal in their potential, but the difference lies in where they are aimed and how far they go. Only a few reach their target, while others fall short. Therefore, although people may start out equal in their nature or initial conditions, their actions and choices make them different from one another.

Douglass argued that there is a hierarchy among individuals, based on their motivation to succeed. A motivated individual who works hard can climb the social ladder, while someone without motivation cannot improve their position. Those who take action and work hard are helped along the way, while those who do not remain stagnant.

The concept of the self-made man originated from Benjamin Franklin's autobiography.[122] In it, he tells the story of how he, the son of a candle maker, became a highly successful

---

[121] Buccola, Nicholas. ""The Essential Dignity of Man as Man": Frederick Douglass on Human Dignity." *American Political Thought* 4.2 (2015): 228-258.

[122] Franklin, Benjamin. *The Autobiography of Benjamin Franklin*. Vol. 41. PF Collier, 1909.

businessman, politician, and diplomat.[123] Franklin painted the pattern of upward mobility for the lowest rung of American society, who, despite all obstacles, climb the social ladder to the highest level and create their own identities, regardless of their family's social status.

The elements that led to their success were their hard work, intelligence, and morality. Franklin also emphasized the importance of personal development. Douglass also noted that a self-made man's social position did not come from his family or external aid, but rather from his own merits. "The self-made man owes nothing to his birth, relations, or friendly surroundings. He is a product of his own work, not of an inherited legacy or early education."

3.1.5.1 Criticism to Self-Made Man Concept

The concept of the self-made man has been a cornerstone of the American Dream and is often associated with entrepreneurship. It is the idea that through hard work, determination, and individualism, anyone can achieve success and wealth. However, this concept can be criticized for its potential negative effects on society and the economy.

The idea of the self-made man promotes an individualistic mindset that can lead to a lack of concern for the well-being of others. This can result in a society that values personal success over the success of the community as a whole. Additionally, it can lead to a culture of greed and a desire for excessive wealth, often at the expense of others.

One of the modern criticisms of the self-made man concept is that it no longer has a place in society, as teamwork is now emphasized more in the US. However, this is an inaccurate

---

[123] Watanabe, Toshio, et al. "Benjamin Franklin: The Self-Made Man as an American Hero." *The American Review* 1977.11 (1977): 219-241.

conclusion. The successes of Apple, Facebook and Google were also achieved through team efforts but there are iconic starters and leaders behind these success stories. These are self-made individuals who created everything from scratch. Every Silicon Valley company has its own self-made man story behind it. Steve Jobs,[124] the founder of Apple, came from a working-class family, and Jeff Bezos[125], the founder of Amazon.com, is the son of a Cuban refugee who worked as a laborer. These individuals took responsibility for their own destiny and pursued their dreams, founding some of the world's largest companies instead of becoming laborers like their fathers.

Another criticism directed at the self-made man concept is that, despite their claim of not receiving help, these individuals have actually been aided by the country. It is hard to imagine Facebook without the internet infrastructure, Ford without highways, or Boeing without engineering schools or steel industry. However, this criticism has a flawed premise. The infrastructure and institutions in America are a service offered to all citizens, and it is not a special aid given to these entrepreneurs.

Although Steve Jobs, Bill Gates, and Mark Zuckerberg all attended good schools, they did not rely on their diplomas to build their careers, as they dropped out of college. Self-made individuals played an important role in the establishment of America, and the current conditions in America still allow an ordinary citizen to become a millionaire in a short amount of time. The internet has even increased the possibilities for this to happen. Thus, the self-made man concept is still relevant in America.

[124] Isaacson, Walter. *Steve Jobs*. Simon & Schuster, 2011.

[125] Sherman, Josepha. *Jeff Bezos: King of Amazon*. Twenty-First Century Books, 2001.

The notion of the self-made man can also have a negative impact on social mobility. This concept assumes that everyone has an equal chance of success, regardless of their socioeconomic background. However, this is not always the case, as many people face systemic barriers that prevent them from achieving their goals.[126] This can lead to a perpetuation of social inequality and a lack of diversity in entrepreneurship.

The idea of the self-made man can be harmful to the environment and other resources. The focus on individualism and success can lead to a disregard for the impact that entrepreneurial activities can have on the environment, as well as other limited resources.

Cornelius Vanderbilt,[127] a self-made man of the 19th century, is often touted as a prime example of American entrepreneurship. Vanderbilt's ruthless tactics and monopolistic practices disrupted the transportation industry and led to the consolidation of power in the hands of a few.

Similarly, Bill Gates, the founder of Microsoft, is often praised for his entrepreneurial spirit and innovation. However, Microsoft's dominance in the tech industry in the 1990s led to accusations of antitrust violations and stifling of competition.[128] This not only disrupted the economy and the tech industry but also impacted the social order by slowing down innovation and access to market for smaller companies and individuals.

---

[126] Neckerman, Kathryn, ed. *Social inequality*. Russell Sage Foundation, 2004.

[127] Stiles, T. J. *The first tycoon: The epic life of Cornelius Vanderbilt*. Knopf, 2009.

[128] Page, William H., and John E. Lopatka. *The Microsoft case: antitrust, high technology, and consumer welfare*. University of Chicago Press, 2009.

In conclusion, while the concept of the self-made man has played a significant role in American entrepreneurship, it is important to recognize the complex and often intertwined factors that contribute to individual success. Doing so facilitates a deeper comprehension of the challenges and opportunities confronting entrepreneurs and aids in fostering a society that is more sustainable and equitable.

3.1.5.2. Self-Made Man Concept in Europe

The concept of the self-made man was a driving force behind the growth of entrepreneurship and innovation in the United States. However, this concept was not prevalent in continental Europe between the 17th century and now.

Firstly, Europe has a long history of class-based societies, where social mobility was often limited by birth and family connections.[129] In many cases, the most successful individuals were those who inherited wealth and social status from their parents. This made it difficult for individuals from lower classes to rise up and achieve success on their own.

The primary reason for this was the strong presence of noble families[130] who held a significant amount of capital and controlled much of the economy. These families tended to invest in their own businesses rather than encouraging outsiders to enter the market.

For example, the Renault family founded the Renault automobile company in France in 1899, which became one of the largest car manufacturers in the world, and the family still

---

[129] Mann, Michael. *The sources of social power: volume 2, the rise of classes and nation-states, 1760-1914*. Vol. 2. Cambridge University Press, 2012.

[130] Dewald, Jonathan. *The European Nobility, 1400-1800*. Vol. 9. Cambridge University Press, 1996.

holds a significant stake in the business today.[131] Similarly, the Philips family founded the Dutch electronics company Philips in 1891, which grew to become a leading producer of consumer electronics and home appliances, and the family has remained influential in the business for generations. The Agnelli family founded the Italian car company Fiat in 1899, and they still hold a significant stake in the company today. The Krupp family founded the German steel company Krupp in 1811, which became one of the largest and most successful industrial conglomerates in Europe, and the family remained in control of the business for over a century. The Rothschild family founded a banking dynasty that began in Frankfurt, Germany in the late 18th century, and the family's financial empire grew to include banks throughout Europe, with a significant influence on global finance. The Guinness family founded the Irish brewery Guinness in 1759, and the family maintained control of the business for generations. The Hermès family founded the French luxury goods company Hermès in 1837, which became famous for its high-quality leather goods and accessories, and the family remained involved in the business for many years. These examples show that noble families in Europe tended to invest in their own businesses and maintain control of them for generations, rather than encouraging outsiders to enter the market and become self-made entrepreneurs.

Secondly, Europe's education system has traditionally focused more on classical knowledge and social etiquette, rather than practical skills and innovation. This has created a culture that values academic achievement and conformity over individual initiative and risk-taking.

As it is mentioned several times in this text, Europe's legal and economic systems have often been less favorable to

---

[131] About Renault, https://www.renault.com.eg/AboutRenault/Renault-history.html, retrieved on September 21, 2023.

entrepreneurs than those in the US. European countries have tended to have more complex regulations and higher taxes, which can make it difficult for new businesses to get off the ground. Additionally, Europe's tradition of state intervention in the economy has sometimes stifled innovation and competition.

In spite of the aforementioned unfavorable conditions in Europe, there were still notable entrepreneurs and inventors who made significant contributions to innovation and entrepreneurship. For instance, Germany's Siemens, Porsche, Daimler, and Benz all founded successful and influential automobile and engineering companies. Additionally, Bach, one of the most famous composers in history, and James Watt, who invented the steam engine, both hailed from Europe. Alan Turing, a British mathematician and computer scientist, made significant contributions to the field of computing, while Antoni Norbert Patek and Adrien Philippe founded the Swiss luxury watch company Patek Philippe in 1839. These examples demonstrate that, while the concept of the self-made man may not have been as prevalent in Europe as in the United States, there were still individuals who were able to overcome the challenges posed by social hierarchies, complex regulations, and high taxes to achieve great success in their respective fields.

Nature gives you the face you have at twenty; it is up to you to merit the face you have at fifty.
Coco Chanel

3.1.6. Social Structure Based on Meritocracy

Meritocracy is an organizational approach in which individuals are promoted to positions based on their talents, knowledge, expertise, and skills.[132] In this organizational approach, merit is the key factor and the most qualified individuals are selected for each position. Another aspect of meritocracy is the absence of favoritism based on other qualities. In other words, a person cannot be promoted to a certain position due to their relationships, acquaintances, or financial connections. In meritocracy, particularly in government administration, more knowledgeable and talented individuals with higher qualifications are selected, and progress and promotions within the organization are based on knowledge, skills, and achievements.

One of the works that defined the framework for meritocracy was "The Rise of Meritocracy"[133] by Michael Young. This book turned meritocracy into a well-known concept worldwide. The book argues against obtaining a position in business, government, education, or science based on family relationships and inspires the formulation "IQ+Effort=Merit."

When the United States was founded, the government organization was a small organization consisting of elected representatives and their assistants. As the government grew, a more sophisticated system had to be established. In 1828, President Andrew Jackson attempted to prevent possible bribery or other problems by rotating bureaucrats in different departments.[134] Later, with each new presidential election, all bureaucrats were fired and new officials were appointed. In

---

[132] Daniels, Norman. "Merit and meritocracy." *Philosophy & Public Affairs* (1978): 206-223.

[133] Young, Michael. *The rise of the meritocracy*. Routledge, 2017.

[134] Nelson, Michael. "A short, ironic history of American national bureaucracy." *The Journal of Politics* 44.3 (1982): 747-778.

1881, after President James Garfield was assassinated by a disgruntled civil servant who was not appointed after the election, an alternative civil servant appointment system was sought.[135] As a result, Chester Alan Arthur began working on a public service reform law called the Pendleton Act.[136] The law was named after its supporter, Senator George H. Pendleton, and became known as the Pendleton Act.

In 1883, the Pendleton Civil Service Reform Act was passed to ensure that appointments in the government would be made based on merit. According to this law, all government officials would be hired through examinations based on merit, and no government official could be dismissed for political reasons. The merit-based system of appointments took away the power of party leaders to appoint officials. The law applied to the federal government, but not to state or local governments. Initially, only a limited number of public servants were hired through the examination system, but eventually, most federal positions were included in the merit-based system.

One of the problems with meritocracy is determining the criteria for determining competence. In other words, it is a problem of determining who will be judged by which standards. It is not helpful to put government officials through a general culture or general aptitude test and rank them according to these tests if the tests are not relevant to the job they will perform. Moreover, some students who perform well on written exams may not be successful in real life because real life requires social skills, problem-solving skills, and initiative. These skills cannot be easily measured through written tests.

---

[135] Uhler, Kevin A. *The demise of patronage: Garfield, the midterm election, and the passage of the Pendleton Civil Service Act*. Diss. The Florida State University, 2011.

[136] Nicole Mitchel, Pendleton Civil Service Act, Amazon Digital Services, 2013.

In addition, those who administer and design the tests must be impartial, unbiased, and objective. However, measuring whether these individuals possess these qualities is a separate problem. The students who receive the highest grades on specific exams are usually those who have previously attended the best schools in the country. After graduating from these schools, they become successful government officials. This process turns out to be a transition from elite families to elite government officials. As a result, the chances of those who do not come from elite families entering the government administration are low.

Despite all these criticisms, in the United States, talent and competence have come to the fore, not only in the public sector but also in every field. The best test of people's abilities is their actual results in their work. When Bill Gates was awarded the contract to write the operating system for IBM, he was a law student at Harvard University with no formal education in computer engineering. However, he was able to secure the job because he had the ability to write computer programs.[137] Similarly, Steve Jobs, despite having no degree, founded one of the world's largest technology companies and gained acceptance through his knowledge and vision. However, he was fired by the board of directors of the company he founded, who found him inadequate.[138] These two examples alone demonstrate how thoroughly meritocracy has become ingrained in American culture.

In recent times, there have been efforts to measure merit not only through exams but also through direct results. The competence and success of company CEOs are measured by

---

[137] Wallace, James, and Jim Erickson. *Hard drive: Bill Gates and the making of the Microsoft empire*. John Wiley & Sons, Inc., 1992.

[138] Young, Jeffrey S., and William L. Simon. *iCon Steve Jobs*. John Wiley & Sons, 2006.

the stock performance of the companies they manage. Similarly, the merit and success of teachers are measured by the achievements of their students in exams.

America has made significant progress by placing the right people in the right positions based on merit. It can be said that merit-based appointments have been made from the early days of the country's founding to the present day. In fact, it can be said that meritocracy began in colonial times before America's establishment. During the period when it was a British colony, administrators with high-level managerial skills were appointed as governors, rather than prominent members of the British Royal family.[139]

3.1.6.1 Criticism to American Social Structure Based on Meritocracy

The concept of meritocracy, or a social structure based on merit and individual achievement, has been touted as a key factor in American entrepreneurship. However, it is not without its criticisms.

One of the main critiques of meritocracy is that it fails to account for systemic inequalities and biases that can prevent certain groups from having equal opportunities to succeed.[140] This can be seen throughout American history, from the exclusion of women and people of color from educational and economic opportunities to the ongoing wage gap between different demographic groups.

For example, despite being one of the wealthiest men in history and a prominent entrepreneur, Andrew Carnegie's

---

[139] Purvis, Thomas L. *Colonial America to 1763*. Infobase Publishing, 2014.

[140] Caliendo, Stephen. *Inequality in America: Race, poverty, and fulfilling democracy's promise*. Routledge, 2021.

success was built on the backs of underpaid and overworked steel workers. He is also criticized for his views on the "Gospel of Wealth,"[141] which argued that the wealthy had a moral obligation to use their wealth for philanthropy rather than addressing the root causes of poverty and inequality.

Another example is the tech industry, which has faced criticism for its lack of diversity and inclusion. While many tech companies tout their merit-based hiring and promotion practices, studies have shown that unconscious biases and systemic barriers often result in homogenous workforces and leadership teams. This can limit innovation and result in products and services that do not reflect the needs and experiences of diverse populations.

In recent years, there has been a growing recognition of the need to address these systemic inequalities and biases in order to truly create a merit-based society. This includes initiatives to increase access to education and economic opportunities for marginalized communities, as well as efforts to promote diversity and inclusion in the workplace.

Ultimately, while meritocracy may be an ideal to strive for, it is important to acknowledge the ways in which systemic biases and inequalities can prevent individuals and groups from achieving their full potential in entrepreneurship and other areas of life.

3.1.6.2. Meritocracy in Europe

The concept of meritocracy, which promotes the selection and advancement of individuals based on their abilities and qualifications, has played a different role in the social structure of Continental Europe compared to the United

---

[141] Carnegie, Andrew HG. *The gospel of wealth, and other timely essays*. Harvard University Press, 1962.

States. While meritocracy has been a fundamental principle in the United States, its influence and implementation in Continental Europe have been more varied and influenced by historical, cultural, and socio-political factors.

In Continental Europe, particularly during the 17th century and the subsequent centuries, the social structure was largely based on a hierarchical system that emphasized hereditary privilege and the noble class.[142] Power and opportunities were often reserved for those born into noble families or belonging to the aristocracy, regardless of their individual talents or qualifications. This entrenched social structure limited the potential for meritocracy to flourish in the same way it did in the United States.

In many European countries, such as France, Germany, and Austria, the rigid social hierarchy and noble class remained influential and held significant power over economic and political affairs. Opportunities for social advancement and access to resources were largely determined by one's family background and connections, rather than individual merit. This resulted in a system that often favored the privileged few and hindered the upward mobility of those without noble lineage.

Additionally, educational systems in Continental Europe[143] often reflected the social structure, with elite institutions catering to the noble class and providing them with superior educational opportunities. The emphasis on pedigree and family ties meant that individuals from less privileged

---

[142] Smith, Stefan Halikoswki. "Demystifying a change in taste: Spices, space, and social hierarchy in Europe, 1380–1750." *The International history review* 29.2 (2007): 237-257.

[143] Maxwell, Claire, and Peter Aggleton, eds. *Elite education: International perspectives*. Routledge, 2015.

backgrounds faced significant barriers to accessing high-quality education and the opportunities it could provide.

However, it is important to mention that Continental Europe is a diverse region with varying degrees of meritocratic practices across countries and time periods. Over time, some European countries began to embrace meritocratic principles and move away from strict social hierarchies. This was particularly evident during the Enlightenment era, which emphasized reason, individualism, and the value of personal achievements.[144] [145]

In more recent history, the impact of meritocracy has become more pronounced in some European countries, particularly in areas such as education and employment. Efforts have been made to create fairer systems that recognize individual talents and qualifications, regardless of social background. Access to education has become more equitable, and efforts have been made to promote equal opportunities for all individuals to pursue their aspirations.

Nevertheless, it is important to acknowledge that the influence of historical social structures and cultural norms can still be seen in certain aspects of Continental European societies today. Family connections, social networks, and inherited wealth continue to play a role in shaping opportunities and outcomes.

In summary, while meritocracy has played a less prominent role in the social structure of Continental Europe compared to the United States, it is a complex and evolving concept that

---

[144] Durant, Will, and Ariel Durant. *The Age of reason begins: a history of European civilization in the period of Shakespeare, Bacon, Montaigne, Rembrandt, Galileo, and Descartes: 1558-1648*. Simon and Schuster, 1961.

[145] Manuel, Frank E. *The age of reason*. Cornell University Press, 2019.

has had varying degrees of influence across different European countries and time periods. The historical prevalence of social hierarchies and the noble class has posed challenges to the widespread implementation of meritocracy. However, as European societies have evolved, efforts have been made to embrace meritocratic principles and create more inclusive systems that recognize individual talents and qualifications.

I am the American Dream. I am the epitome of what the American Dream basically said. It said you could come from anywhere and be anything you want in this country. That's exactly what I've done.
Whoopi Goldberg

3.1.7. American Dream

According to the authors of the book "Chasing the American Dream,"[146] Rank, Hirsch, and Foster, the American Dream defines America at its core. It is a life of prosperity for those who wish to work hard and take advantage of opportunities. America is synonymous with equal opportunity, and is a country where hard work and a combination of talents can lead to personal success. Although everyone's dream is different, the existence of this dream remains constant.

One of the significant differences between Europeans and Americans is that Europe's class-based society does not allow for much mobility between classes. As mentioned earlier, Europe has a class-based society due to its long history of feudalism, monarchy, and aristocracy, which entrenched social hierarchies and inequalities. In America, the absence of a class-based society has allowed everyone to believe that they can achieve great things. The actual existence of equal opportunity has provided every American with an ideal for a happy and successful life. Americans believe that they can achieve their goals in proportion to their hard work and creativity. Although the term "American Dream" emerged in the 1930s, the belief in the American Dream existed in the earliest European immigrants.

The American Dream[147] is a concept that is intimately linked with the individual and is synonymous with the Declaration of Independence. Seeing people at the lowest level of society rise to the highest levels by working hard has given those who are part of this society the idea that they too can achieve great success through hard work. Even people living at the lower

---

[146] Mark Robert Rank, Thomas A. Hirschl, Kirk A. Foster, **Chasing the American Dream**, Oxford University Press, 2014.

[147] Jim Cullen, **The American dream: a short history of an idea that shaped a nation,** Oxford University Press US, 2004, sf. 3.

levels of society without education can rise through the ranks based on their talents, accomplishments, and the quality of their work. This widespread belief in America has given people the American Dream, and this dream has inspired them to take action.

The Protestant work ethic[148] and religious beliefs have also supported the American Dream and the work ethic. The belief that hard work is valuable and that earnings should be saved rather than spent has led to both increased productivity and the accumulation of capital.

The American Dream is a national phenomenon in America. For every American citizen, it represents democratic ideals, great achievements, and wealth. James Truslow Adams first expressed it in 1931. Every citizen can achieve a better, richer, and happier life, regardless of their level. The American Dream is expressed in the second sentence of the Declaration of Independence: "We hold these truths to be self-evident, that all men are created equal, that they are endowed by their Creator with certain unalienable Rights, that among these are Life, Liberty and the pursuit of Happiness."

The concept of the American Dream may have only been coined in the 20th century, but it has been experienced through four centuries of the continent's history, including its discovery, westward expansion, statehood, independence from British rule, the emancipation of slaves, and broad economic growth stories. The American Dream represents a country where one advances in life solely through talent and energy, rather than through political connections or family wealth. According to the American Dream, everyone has the right to raise and educate their children and to be given all

---

[148] Giorgi, Liana, and Catherine Marsh. "The Protestant work ethic as a cultural phenomenon." *European Journal of Social Psychology* 20.6 (1990): 499-517.

possible career opportunities, regardless of social class, religion, language, race, or ethnic background.

The American Dream embodies the idea that life can be richer and better for everyone, depending on their abilities or achievements. It is a dream of a social order where each individual can reach their innate potential and be recognized by others for what they are, regardless of their birth or social position. James Truslow Adams first defined the American Dream in his book The Epic of America,[149] which he wrote in 1931. He said that the American Dream is "that dream of a land in which life should be better and richer and fuller for everyone, with opportunity for each according to ability or achievement. It is a difficult dream for the European upper classes to interpret adequately, and too many of us ourselves have grown weary and mistrustful of it. It is not a dream of motor cars and high wages merely, but a dream of social order in which each man and each woman shall be able to attain to the fullest stature of which they are innately capable, and be recognized by others for what they are, regardless of the fortuitous circumstances of birth or position."

The American Dream can be seen in the speeches of community leaders like Martin Luther King and the writings of the founding fathers like Benjamin Franklin. Even minimum-wage workers, high school students, or single mothers trying to raise a family have their own great aspirations, a belief that one day they will succeed greatly, and the expression of this hope helps to make the American Dream visible.

The American Dream can also be described as a journey, from one point or level to another. It may involve moving to a new place, climbing the ladder from the lowest to the highest

---

[149] James Truslow Adams, **The Epic of America**, Blue Ribbon Books, New York, 1931.

position in a particular field, or even achieving stardom in a completely different area. The American Dream can take place over an individual's entire lifetime or even span generations, with a father's dream being inherited by his son and even his grandson. For Americans, individual goals under the umbrella of the American Dream serve as a compass.

While James Truslow Adams defined the American Dream as a dream of a social order in which everyone can be successful, the dream is often criticized for having many exceptions. Entrepreneurial billionaires like Cornelius Vanderbilt, Rockefeller, and Andrew Carnegie have frequently been accused of obtaining their wealth through monopolies or exploiting workers. However, just as a coin has two sides, every person has good and bad qualities. Ultimately, entrepreneurs pursuing the American Dream may sometimes resort to Machiavellian tactics to achieve success, but they still operate within the system.

Critics argue that actual discrimination based on race, class, and gender in America hinders the American Dream. However, examples like Barack Obama becoming president, Steve Jobs and Mark Zuckerberg becoming millionaires at a young age despite dropping out of college, Arnold Schwarzenegger becoming a film star and politician despite his Austrian accent, and Tiger Woods becoming a legendary golf star despite being black demonstrate that such criticism may not be valid.

Donald Barlett and James Steele suggest that the American Dream has been betrayed, pointing out that American policies are causing the middle class to lose their opportunities.[150] As

---

[150] Donald Barlett, James B. Steele, **The Betrayal of the American Dream,** Public Affairs, 2012.

Americans shift from production to design and research and development, jobs in the factories where the middle class works are decreasing. The famous Apple iPhone, for instance, is designed in California but produced in China. However, this critique may be misplaced since the middle class can still pursue their dreams by utilizing their creativity and talents. Despite the narrowing of work opportunities for the middle class, this does not prevent them from climbing the ladder and joining the upper class.

America's most important feature in this sense is its ability to protect and sustain itself despite some deviations from its ideals. Over time, America abolished slavery, granted citizenship rights to African Americans, and provided opportunities for minority groups to be represented at the highest levels. The American Dream continues to be functional today, as demonstrated by the founders of WhatsApp, who became billionaires in just a few years. Jan Koum and Brian Acton, who came to America to work from Ukraine, founded the company with $250,000 in capital in 2009, and it was sold for $19 billion in 2014[151]. After starting at Yahoo, Koum decided to develop a secure and simple communication application, and his partnership with Brian Acton turned it into a global success. Even this small story proves that the American Dream is still valid even for the newest immigrants.

3.1.7.1. Criticism to the Concept of American Dream

The American Dream, the idea that anyone can achieve success through hard work and determination, has long been held up as a cornerstone of American society. However, in

---

[151] Parmy Olson, "Facebook Closes $19 Billion WhatsApp Deal," Forbes, October 6, 2014, https://www.forbes.com/sites/parmyolson/2014/10/06/facebook-closes-19-billion-whatsapp-deal/?sh=7b69869a5c66.

recent years, there has been growing criticism of the American Dream and its role in entrepreneurship.

One of the primary criticisms is that the American Dream is a myth. While hard work and determination can certainly lead to success, there are many other factors that come into play, such as access to education, social connections, and economic opportunities. The American Dream, then, can be seen as a way of justifying social inequality, by suggesting that those who have not achieved success simply haven't worked hard enough.

Furthermore, the pursuit of the American Dream can be seen as a barrier to entrepreneurship. Many people are so focused on achieving financial success and social status that they are unwilling to take risks or pursue unconventional paths. This can lead to a lack of innovation and creativity in the business world.

Historically, this can be seen in the way that certain groups, such as women and people of color, have been systematically excluded from the benefits of the American Dream. For example, women were not granted the right to vote until 1920,[152] and even then, faced significant social and economic barriers to achieving success. Similarly, people of color faced discrimination in housing, employment, and education for many years, making it much harder for them to achieve the American Dream.

Moreover, the American Dream can be seen as a form of individualism that prioritizes personal success over the

---

[152] Brown, Jennifer K. "The Nineteenth Amendment and women's equality." *The Yale Law Journal* 102.8 (1993): 2175-2204.

common good.[153] This can lead to a lack of investment in public goods, such as education, healthcare, and infrastructure, which are necessary for a healthy and prosperous society.

In conclusion, while the American Dream has long been held up as a defining feature of American society, it is not without its flaws. By perpetuating the myth of meritocracy, the American Dream can be seen as a way of justifying social inequality and excluding certain groups from achieving success. Moreover, the individualistic focus of the American Dream can lead to a lack of investment in public goods, ultimately harming society as a whole.

3.1.7.2. Quest of an European Dream

The concept of the "American Dream" does not have a direct counterpart in Europe due to the continent's rich tapestry of diverse cultures, histories, values, and socio-economic structures inherent to its numerous nations. However, through various epochs, several ideals and themes within Europe could be loosely equated to the American Dream, each with its own specific context and nuances.

In the 17th and 18th centuries, Europe underwent a period known as the Enlightenment,[154] marked by a surge in ideals focusing on reason, individualism, and progress. Philosophies that emerged during this transformative era influenced not only societal norms but also the foundations of governance and the recognition of individual rights. This was a period when a European form of a "dream" began to crystallize, characterized by an emphasis on the pursuit of knowledge,

---

[153] Gaur, Bhawna. "The Dark Side of Leadership." *Global Leadership Perspectives on Industry, Society, and Government in an Era of Uncertainty*. IGI Global, 2023. 176-201.

[154] Outram, Dorinda. *The enlightenment*. Cambridge University Press, 2019.

the quest for freedom, and a commitment to progress, which can be considered analogous to the American Dream in its aspirations for individual betterment and societal advancement.

Within the myriad cultures and societies of Europe, the quest for social mobility and ascent has long been a notable motif, comparable to certain aspects of the American Dream. This quest is deeply intertwined with the individual's desire to rise above the circumstances of their birth and achieve a higher status within the societal and economic hierarchies through merit, effort, and accomplishment.

In various European societies, this pursuit is marked by an emphasis on education and intellectual cultivation as principal means of elevating one's social standing. The acquisition of knowledge and skills is viewed not merely as a path to personal enlightenment but as a gateway to occupational advancement and economic prosperity. This aspiration for enhanced societal position often implies a transcending of class boundaries and the overcoming of socio-economic constraints.

However, the European perspective on social mobility is typically imbued with a greater focus on communal welfare and societal equilibrium. The desire for personal advancement is often balanced with a commitment to social responsibility and a consideration for the collective well-being of the community.[155] This contrasts with the American Dream's more individual-centric ethos, which predominantly values personal success and economic attainment.

The Welfare State Model, particularly prominent in the post-World War II 20th-century European landscape, represents another parallel. This model prioritizes the provision of equal opportunities, comprehensive social protections, and

---

[155] Outram, Dorinda. *The enlightenment*. Cambridge University Press, 2019.

enhancement of the quality of life for all citizens. The underlying ideals of social equity and accessibility of opportunities and essential services embedded in this model echo the American Dream's promise of improved life circumstances through individual endeavor and resilience.

With the formation of the European Union, a new set of shared values and principles was introduced, championing peace, prosperity, and unity amongst its member nations. The notion of a harmonious, affluent, and peaceful conglomerate of nations underpins a collective "European dream," a unified aspiration for a better collective future.

While each of these European "counterparts" is deeply intertwined with its respective historical, cultural, and socio-political fabric, they distinctly vary from the American Dream. The latter is typically characterized by a strong sense of individualism, the pursuit of economic success, and upward mobility, often manifested in the acquisition of personal wealth and property. Conversely, European ideals are more likely to embody a holistic vision of collective well-being, societal evolution, and intellectual enlightenment, emphasizing communal values and social equity.

To be successful you have to be selfish, or else you never achieve. And once you get to your highest level, then you have to be unselfish. Stay reachable. Stay in touch. Don't isolate.
Michael Jordan

3.1.8. American Individualism

There is a fundamental relationship between American thinking and individualism. Individualism emphasizes the individual's goals and desires, and focuses on their freedom and ability to stand on their own two feet. The classless structure in America, equality before the law, and equal opportunity have also contributed to the development of American individualism. The democracy based on the proposition that "there can be no equality without freedom, and no freedom without equality" has also shaped American individualism. Alexis de Tocqueville noted that equality gave rise to individuals who could not dominate others, but were self-sufficient.[156]

Many of the founders of the American Republic were examples of leaders who were interested in individualism. Thomas Jefferson, who wrote the Declaration of Independence, included views that could be considered the cornerstone of individualism in this document:

"We hold these truths to be self-evident, that all men are created equal, that they are endowed by their Creator with certain unalienable Rights, that among these are Life, Liberty and the pursuit of Happiness. That to secure these rights, Governments are instituted among Men, deriving their just powers from the consent of the governed. That whenever any Form of Government becomes destructive of these ends, it is the Right of the People to alter or to abolish it, and to institute new Government, laying its foundation on such principles and organizing its powers in such form, as to them shall seem most likely to effect their Safety and Happiness."[157]

---

[156] Alexis de Tocqueville, **Democracy in America**, Penguin Classics, 2003.

[157] Thomas Jefferson, **The Declaration of Independence**, http://www.ushistory.org/Declaration/document/index.htm, (24.07.2012).

The concept of equality in the above text can be considered the beginning of individual freedom. Because if everyone is not equal, it is possible for some individuals or groups to dominate others. Jefferson made self-governing society an ideal for years of his life. He claimed that the best way to defend freedom was to have educated people involved in the governing process.

In his work "Self-Reliance," Ralph Waldo Emerson wrote, "No government or church can explain a man's heart to him, and so each individual must resist institutional authority. ...To believe your own thought, to believe that what is true for you in your private heart is true for all men, — that is genius.... A man is relieved and gay when he has put his heart into his work and done his best; but what he has said or done otherwise shall give him no peace. It is a deliverance which does not deliver. In the attempt his genius deserts him; no muse befriends; no invention, no hope."[158] Emerson rejected any kind of group proposal or tradition that would control or surrender the individual. The individuals must follow their own hearts.

Ralph Waldo Emerson also said, "Whilst thus the world will be whole and refuses to be disparted, we seek to act partially, to sunder, to appropriate..."[159] implying that while the world does not want individuals to be separate from the whole, being an individual means being separate from the whole.

John Winthrop (1588-1649) was one of the first Puritans to arrive on the shores of America. He was also the first governor elected to the Massachusetts Bay Colony. Before his ship docked in Salem in 1630, Winthrop gave a sermon titled "A

---

[158] Emerson, Ralph Waldo, and Richard Wulf. *Self-reliance*. Caxton Society, 1909.

[159] Ralph Waldo Emerson, Essays, http://www.gutenberg.org/etext/2944, (24.12.2011).

Model of Christian Charity," in which he first described the concept of a "City set upon a hill."[160] This city is the utopian city that the Puritans sought to find. Winthrop's words in the sermon explain the way of life he wanted in America:

> "......*we must uphold a familiar Commerce together in all meekness, gentleness, patience, and liberality, we must delight in each other, make others' conditions our own, rejoice together, mourn together, labor, and suffer together, always having before our eyes our Commission and Community in the work, our Community as members of the same body....*"

Winthrop's words reveal that the American ideal is not founded on individualism but rather on communal living. Analyzing from a holistic perspective reveals that the reality of American society is constituted by individuals expressing themselves within a collective social structure.

The Puritans were not concerned with material wealth. Their criterion for success was a truly moral and spiritually high life. During Winthrop's twelve-term governorship, he was a wealthy man who used his own wealth for public purposes. Toward the end of his life, he had almost depleted his wealth and was forced to resign from the governorship. Under Winthrop's leadership, the Puritans' initiative was the first utopian quest in American history. Although this utopian quest was unsuccessful, the spirit of the utopian quest has become a part of American culture.

According to Winthrop, natural liberty, which allows one to do as they please, is as harmful as it is beneficial. He defined moral freedom, on the other hand, as being simple, good, and honest.

---

[160] Parker, Michael. *John Winthrop: founding the city upon a hill*. Routledge, 2013.

Alexis de Tocqueville, a French political thinker, published his book Democracy in America in 1835, after traveling through America. It is considered one of the first works in sociology and political science. Tocqueville masterfully discusses egalitarian democracy and individualism in America in his book:

> "Individualism is a novel expression, to which a novel idea has given birth. Our fathers were only acquainted with egotism. Egotism is a passionate and exaggerated love of self, which leads a man to connect everything with his own person, and to prefer himself to everything in the world. Individualism is a mature and calm feeling, which disposes each member of the community to sever himself from the mass of his fellow-creatures; and to draw apart with his family and his friends; so that, after he has thus formed a little circle of his own, he willingly leaves society at large to itself."[161]

Tocqueville distinguishes between selfishness and individualism. Selfishness is greed, while individualism means maturely looking out for one's interests within society. This perspective complements Winthrop's.

As societal conditions become more equal, the number of people who cannot dominate others, are not too rich or too powerful increases. However, these people have received adequate education and have a life where they can satisfy their own desires. They owe nothing to anyone and expect nothing from anyone else; they have developed a habit of thinking that they can stand alone. They tend to believe that their destiny is in their own hands. Democracy not only makes

---

[161] De Tocqueville, Alexis. *Democracy in America-Vol. I. and II.* Read Books Ltd, 2015.

everyone forget their ancestors, but also separates everyone from their own race's future and contemporaries.

Tocqueville argues that the equality brought about by democracy prevents different segments of society from exerting dominance over one another. Educated and equal individuals lack the shortcomings that would allow others to control them, and they do not rely on others for anything.

The greatest advantage of Americans was their transition to democracy without a revolution; they were not made equal, but born equal. Tocqueville extensively compares America to Europe, especially France, where the struggle to transition to democracy under class-based structures and monarchic rule was ongoing. In contrast, immigrants to America were able to transition to democracy as soon as they were freed from British rule. Each immigrant from Europe to America was an equal individual.

In his work "Poor Richard's Almanack,"[162] Benjamin Franklin included many sections emphasizing individualism, such as "God helps those who help themselves" and "Early to bed and early to rise, makes a man healthy, wealthy, and wise." Franklin emphasized that individuals can take the initiative and control their own destinies. According to those influenced by Franklin, the focus was on personal development, and establishing a broader social context was difficult. By the end of the 18th century, social welfare would emerge on its own through those who pursued their own interests.

Individualism has become a symbolic key term for a broad ideological meaning, including the natural rights philosophy of the American Declaration of Independence, the belief in free enterprise, and the American Dream. Individualism

---

[162] Franklin, Benjamin. *Poor Richard's almanack*. Barnes & Noble Publishing, 2004.

concerns the practical or near-future realization of humanity's progress in a society where equal individual rights, limited government, free enterprise, natural justice with equal opportunity, individual freedom, moral development, and seriousness of purpose converge spontaneously.

Yehosua Arieli regards American individualism as a symbol of national identity: "Individualism provided behavioral patterns and aspirations to the nation through the rationalization of its distinctive attitudes. It bestowed unity and a perspective of progress upon the past, present, and future. Individualism indicated the unique social organizational ideal of the nation. Most importantly, individualism expressed that the most specific quality of national consciousness is universality and idealism."[163]

An article by Grabb, Baer, and Curtis in the Canadian Journal of Sociology revisits American individualism through historical records.[164] The article challenges S.M. Lipset's famous thesis that "the American dominant value system is shaped by the fundamental events of the American Revolution." According to Lipset and many other writers, American individualism is based on a self-interested concept of personal freedom. They argue that the American value system is based on an individualistic pursuit of self-interest in the nation's founding.

However, many of these same writers also describe responsible groups of people united in the ideal of

---

[163] Yehoshua Arieli, **Individualism and Nationalism in American Ideology,** Penguin, 1966, s.345-346

[164164] Edward Grabb, Douglas Baer, and James Curtis, The Origins of American Individualism: Reconsidering the Historical Evidence, **Canadian Journal of Sociology,** 24, 4, 1999, s.511-533.

Revolutionary American society. This portrayal of the American value system emphasizes civic responsibility and respect for the rights of others, elevating these concepts. In reality, the realization of freedom depends on citizens sacrificing their own interests for the good of society. Therefore, it is not possible to see American individualism solely as a self-interested individualism. This individualism is based on the protection of collective interests. Within this collective attitude, individuals do not disappear, but rather exist through their individual contributions to the whole.

Republican individualism, which emphasizes high levels of social responsibility, was particularly widespread during the American Revolution. This form of individualism was celebrated among national elites, particularly revolutionary leaders. It is questionable how well revolutionary leaders represented the American people at the time. However, it is also reasonable to assume that the thoughts of this group, which came to power through elections and votes, were approved by the people.

Another question regarding individualism is how well the general public understood the concept during the period in which Republican individualism was celebrated. It is known that during that time, the majority of the population was illiterate. However, there are two groups of records on this subject. The first is records based on observations by the founders and people in their circles, and the second is records that include observations by literate people from the public.

All of these factors bring a new perspective to the classic definition of American individualism. American culture experienced a form of small-town community life during the Revolution. The concept of community refers to a group of people who live together, are organized for a specific purpose, and have a high level of loyalty to one another.

As the concept of American individualism continues to be examined from a historical perspective, it also undergoes scrutiny in light of the realities of the 21st century. Two writers from the National Review, Richard Lowry and Ramesh Ponnuru, list the values that America must preserve: America must preserve its unique status, individual freedom, individualism, democracy, and openness. "America is more individualistic than any society in the world."[165]

Sociology professor Claude Fisher from the University of Berkeley questions the traditional views above in the light of his research and comes to surprising conclusions.[166] According to Fisher, there is evidence that Americans are not more individualistic. Fisher argues that the definition of individualism includes prioritizing personal freedom. Prioritizing freedom means valuing awareness against the dominant demands of individuals' interests, objectives, authorities, traditions, feudal lords, churches, states, bosses, and patriarchal family heads.

The International Social Survey Program (ISSP) has conducted research on individualism and similar values in different societies. The results of ISSP research show that Americans were less individualistic than other societies in the early 21st century. A 2006 ISSP survey asked questions about individualism and collectivism levels in different countries by asking the following questions: "In general, do you strictly adhere to laws, or are there situations where people may need to follow their own decisions at the expense of breaking

---

[165] Richard ve Ramesh Ponnuru. "An Exceptional Debate: The Obama Administration's Assault on American identity." **National Review,** 8 Mart 2010, Cilt.62, Sayı.2, s.18-20.

[166] Claude Fischer, American individualism – really? The evidence that we are not who we think we are, http://blogs.berkeley.edu/2010/04/20/american-individualism-%E2%80%93-really, (30.08.2011).

laws?" The answers to this question given by different nations are shown in the below figure.

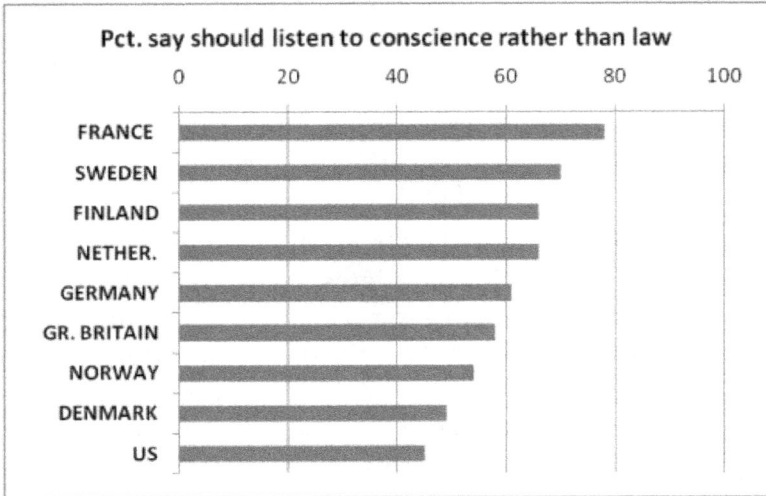

Figure 1: Percentage of people who consider their own conscious choice over the law.)

Source: Claude Fisher, Made in America, Notes on American life from American history. http://madeinamericathebook.wordpress.com/?s=individualism, 30 Ağustos 2011.

According to the chart, Americans try to prioritize the law above their personal interests in comparison to European societies.

Despite Emerson's calls for individuals to resist group and nationalist pressures, contemporary American society presents a different picture. In a study conducted in 2003, participants were asked to express their opinion on the statement, "People should support their country even when their country is wrong." As seen in Figure 3 below, Americans appear to prioritize national interests over their own independent evaluations.

Pct. say should NOT support country if it is wrong

	0	20	40	60	80
FINLAND					
GR. BRITAIN					
SWEDEN					
GERMANY (W.)					
FRANCE					
DENMARK					
AUSTRIA					
US					

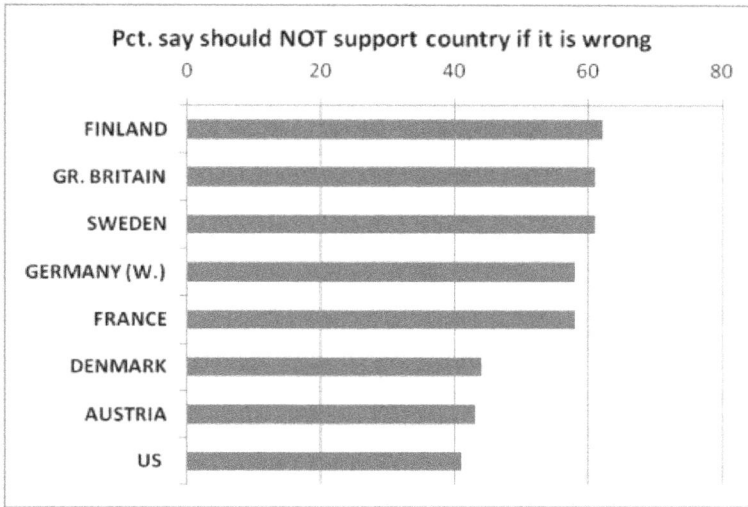

Figure 2: Percentage of people who would not support their country when they believe it is wrong.

Source: Claude Fisher, Made in America, Notes on American life from American history.

http://madeinamericathebook.wordpress.com/?s=individualism, 30 Ağustos 2011.

It's crucial to know that "American Individualism" and "Individualism" aren't the same things. When we say "American Individualism," it means how the idea of being independent and free plays out in America, reflecting national values and conditions. Think of it this way: "Nationalism" usually means putting the country's needs above one's own needs. So, "Nationalist Individualism" is like being free and independent while also caring about the country's needs. Even though America is home to people from many backgrounds, everyone has come together to create a unique society. In this society, people value their individual freedoms but unite when dealing with international matters. American Individualism is special because it is shaped by the unique situations and values found in the United States; it's not just about love for one's country. This special form of individualism is often highlighted and viewed differently when researchers compare the U.S. to other countries.

Americans really appreciate the freedoms they have, like the freedom to speak their mind, keep their lives private, and start their own businesses. They respect the law because they believe that the legal system is there to protect these freedoms, even if it means following laws they don't like.

Even if Americans believe that some of the international actions taken by their country are wrong, like going to war for resources or being the only country with nuclear weapons, they still stand by it. They think that what's good for the country is also good for their personal freedoms. This might seem like they are saying one thing and doing another, but it's a practical way of thinking and suits its purpose well. Starting a business, or entrepreneurship, happens when people, who have their own dreams and goals, operate within a system that society supports. This system lets them acquire what they need, sell their products, and solve disagreements. If everyone just did what they wanted, it would lead to a lot of confusion and disorder. So, following societal rules is really important for individuals to succeed.

In America, the emphasis is both on personal freedom and on working together, which is a good environment for coming up with new ideas and starting successful projects. Unlike societies that only focus on everyone working together or on extreme individualism, the balance in America between these two aspects is a big advantage. This mixture of valuing independence and cooperation makes America fertile ground for the growth of creativity and innovative ideas.

3.1.8.1. Criticism to American Individualism

American individualism has been praised as the driving force behind American entrepreneurship and innovation, but it also has its critics who argue that it can lead to negative consequences.

One criticism of American individualism is that it can lead to a lack of community and social responsibility. In a society that values individual achievement above all else, there is a risk of neglecting the needs of the collective. This can manifest in various ways, from social inequality to environmental degradation.

Historically, the industrial revolution in America is a prime example of how unchecked individualism can lead to negative consequences.[167] During this period, entrepreneurs were able to exploit workers and resources without much regulation or concern for the broader social impact. As a result, workers were subjected to harsh conditions and the environment was degraded, leading to long-term consequences for both human health and the natural world.

Another criticism of American individualism is that it can lead to a narrow focus on short-term goals rather than long-term sustainability.[168] When the focus is on individual achievement and success, there can be a lack of consideration for the broader impact of actions on future generations or the environment.

For example, the boom and bust cycles of the American economy, particularly in the tech industry, can be attributed in

---

[167] Eidlin, Barry. "Class vs. special interest: labor, power, and politics in the United States and Canada in the twentieth century." *Politics & Society* 43.2 (2015): 181-211.

[168] Wu, Lin, et al. "Short-term versus long-term benefits: Balanced sustainability framework and research propositions." *Sustainable Production and Consumption* 11 (2017): 18-30.

part to a culture of individualism that prioritizes short-term gains over long-term sustainability.[169] Startups may prioritize rapid growth and profits over concerns about long-term environmental or social impact.

In addition, American individualism can also lead to a lack of collaboration and cooperation among entrepreneurs, which can hinder innovation and progress. While competition can drive innovation, it can also lead to duplication of effort and a lack of coordination.

One historical example of this is the so-called "war of the currents" between Thomas Edison and George Westinghouse in the late 19th century. The two entrepreneurs were in fierce competition to establish their respective electrical systems as the dominant technology. The result was a long and costly battle that did little to advance the technology as a whole, but instead served to enrich the individual entrepreneurs.

In conclusion, while American individualism has been celebrated as a cornerstone of American entrepreneurship, it is not without its flaws. A lack of community responsibility, a narrow focus on short-term goals, and a lack of collaboration can all have negative consequences for society, the environment, and even the success of individual entrepreneurs in the long term.

3.1.8.2. Individual Goals and Dreams in Europe
The concept of the "American Dream" has been a powerful narrative in the United States, representing the belief that through hard work, determination, and individual aspirations, anyone can achieve success and upward social mobility. In Continental Europe, while there are parallel ideas

---

[169] Van Lange, Paul AM, and Jeff A. Joireman. "How we can promote behavior that serves all of us in the future." *Social Issues and Policy Review* 2.1 (2008): 127-157.

of individual dreams and goals, the context and manifestation of these aspirations have been influenced by different historical, cultural, and socio-economic factors.

In Continental Europe, particularly during the 17th century and beyond, the social structure was often characterized by a more rigid class system and a stronger influence of traditional social hierarchies. The emphasis on social status, family background, and inherited privileges meant that opportunities for individual advancement and the pursuit of personal dreams were often limited for those outside the established elite.

However, it is important to recognize that individuals in Continental Europe have long held their own dreams and goals, which have often been deeply intertwined with cultural and intellectual pursuits. In the business world, European entrepreneurs and innovators have followed their ambitions, aiming to create successful enterprises and leave a lasting impact. For example, in the 19th century, Gustave Eiffel, a French civil engineer, pursued his dream of constructing monumental structures, leading to the creation of the iconic Eiffel Tower in Paris.[170]

While the idea of the "American Dream" has been deeply ingrained in the cultural fabric of the United States, Europe has often approached the concept of individual dreams and goals from a different perspective. The focus on collective welfare, social cohesion, and public goods has been more prominent in European societies in the second half of 20th century. This emphasis has led to robust social welfare systems, accessible healthcare, and comprehensive education, which aim to provide opportunities and support for

---

[170] Bernard Marrey, *The Extraordinary Life and Work of Monsieur Gustave Eiffel, the Engineer Who Built the Statue of Liberty, the Porto Bridge, the Nice Observatory, the ... the Panama Locks, the Eiffel Tower, etc.*, Graphite Publications, January 1, 1984.

individuals to pursue their ambitions within a broader societal context.

In recent years, Europe has also witnessed a shift towards fostering entrepreneurial ecosystems and supporting innovation and individual initiatives. Start-up hubs[171] have emerged in cities like Berlin,[172] London, and Stockholm,[173] nurturing a culture of innovation and encouraging individuals to pursue their entrepreneurial dreams.

However, it is essential to acknowledge that cultural and structural factors continue to influence the manifestation of individual dreams and goals in Continental Europe. Family ties, social networks, and institutional barriers can still shape opportunities and aspirations. The influence of historical social hierarchies and cultural norms can sometimes create a sense of stability and continuity, which can both enable and constrain individual ambitions.

In summary, while the idea of the "American Dream" may have a distinct resonance in the United States, individuals in Continental Europe have also held their own dreams and goals, albeit within different societal contexts. The European version of the American Dream is emerging.[174] European business leaders and literary works provide examples of individuals pursuing their aspirations, often grappling with societal constraints and questioning the consequences of their

---

[171] Koch, Malina. "Tech Start-up Internationalisation: Development of an internationalisation model for born global web-based tech start-ups from European start-up hubs." (2017).

[172] Hall, Fred. *The rise of startup hubs in Europe: a qualitative study on the factors contributing to Berlin's rise as a european startup hub*. Diss. 2016.

[173] Marie, Luzia. "The Dynamics of European Startup Hubs." (2016).

[174] Rifkin, Jeremy. *The European dream: How Europe's vision of the future is quietly eclipsing the American dream*. John Wiley & Sons, 2013.

actions. The European approach to individual dreams and goals often balances the pursuit of personal fulfillment with collective welfare, reflecting a different cultural and historical landscape.

Ultimately, it might be apt to conceptualize the European Union as a semblance of a 'United States of Europe,'[175] representing a collective of nations, akin to the states in the U.S., each contributing to a federated whole. In various domains and disciplines, the European Union seems to be converging towards parallels with the United States.

---

[175] Joseph J. C. Hobbs, Fundamentals of World Regional Geography (Cengage, 2017), 114.

We don't need a melting pot in this country, folks. We need a salad bowl. In a salad bowl, you put in the different things. You want the vegetables - the lettuce, the cucumbers, the onions, the green peppers - to maintain their identity. You appreciate differences.
Jane Elliot

3.1.9. The American Melting Pot

Immigrants from very diverse ethnic backgrounds have formed a nation with new values, which have shaped the American mindset. Jean de Crévecoeur, a French-born thinker, analyzed the formation of the New American Nation in his book "Letters from an American Farmer."[176] This book was also the first work to define the values and way of life of the entire American people.

Jean de Crévecoeur (1735-1813) was born in Normandy, France. In 1755, he emigrated to the New France region of North America. He joined the French army and fought in the French-Indian War. In 1759, he moved to New York State, became an American citizen, took the name John Hector St. John, and married an American woman. He bought a large farm in Orange County and, in addition to farming, made observations about the emergence of American society and life in the American colonies.[177]

In 1782, he wrote a book called "Letters from an American Farmer," a collection of articles, in London. This book was the first literary work by an American writer to gain success in Europe. Crévecoeur was the first author to describe Americans to Europeans. He described how Americans lived by principles of equal opportunity and self-determination. His work provided insights into the understanding of American identity in the New World. He defined America not as a regional colony but as a country.

> *He (an emigrant) is arrived on a new continent; a modern society offers itself to his contemplation, different from what he had hitherto seen. It is not composed, as in Europe, of*

---

[176] de Crevoecoeur, J. Hector St John. *Letters from an American Farmer*. Prabhat Prakashan, 2021.

[177] Mitchell, Julia Post. *St. Jean de Crèvecoeur*. Columbia University Press, 1916.

great lords who possess everything, and of a herd of people who have nothing. Here are no aristocratical families, no courts, no kings, no bishops, no ecclesiastical dominion, no invisible power giving to a few a very visible one; no great manufacturers employing thousands, no great refinements of luxury. The rich and the poor are not so far removed from each other as they are in Europe.[178]

Americans worked a great deal harder than the home Englishmen; for there he told us, that they have no trees to cut down, no fences to make, no negroes to buy and to clothe."

His famous quote "He is arrived on a new continent..." emphasizes that there is no class structure in America. He notes that there are no capitalists, feudal lords, or enslaved Europeans. Additionally, he underscores that Americans work very hard to build everything from scratch.

"What should we American farmers be without the distinct possession of that soil? It feeds, it clothes us, from it we draw even a great exuberancy, our best meat, our richest drink, the very honey of our bees comes from this. privileged spot. No wonder we should thus cherish its possession, no wonder that so many Europeans who have never been able to say that such portion of land was theirs, cross the Atlantic to realise that happiness.[179]

Crevecoeur emphasizes the importance of land ownership and the connection between American farmers and the soil,

---

[178] de Crevoecoeur, J. Hector St John. *Letters from an American Farmer*. Prabhat Prakashan, 2021, pg 16.

[179] de Crevoecoeur, J. Hector St John. *Letters from an American Farmer*. Prabhat Prakashan, 2021, pg. 20.

which he views as the source of their livelihood and happiness.

> *This formerly rude soil has been converted by my father into a pleasant farm, and in return it has established all our rights; on it is founded our rank, our freedom, our power as citizens, our importance as inhabitants of such a district. These images I must confess I always behold with pleasure, and extend them as far as my imagination can reach: for this is what may be called the true and the only philosophy of an American farmer.*[180]

In Europe, it was almost impossible for a poor person to become a landowner, but immigrants who settled in America were able to acquire land much more easily compared to Europe. Land ownership allowed them to earn a living through hard work while also granting them the right to live as honorable citizens.

According to Crévecoeur, Americans are agriculturalists who inhabit an immense territory connected by highways or navigable rivers, and whose delicate ties to a moderate government are reinforced by their collective respect for laws that they believe to be fair to all. Crévecoeur emphasizes that in America, the legal system treats everyone equally, unlike in Europe where judges show different treatment to the rich and poor, and this accepted judicial process has led Americans to be attached to their country.

> *We are all animated with the spirit of an industry which is unfettered and unrestrained, because each person works for himself. If he travels through our rural districts he views not the hostile castle, and the haughty mansion, contrasted with the clay- built hut and miserable cabin, where cattle and men*

---

[180] de Crevoecoeur, J. Hector St John. *Letters from an American Farmer*. Prabhat Prakashan, 2021, pg 18.

help to keep each other warm, and dwell in meanness, smoke, and indigence.[181]

Crévecoeur emphasizes that the destiny of all Americans is to earn their own living through work.

In this great American asylum, the poor of Europe have by some means met together, and in consequence of various causes; to what purpose should they ask one another what countrymen they are? Alas, two thirds of them had no country. Can a wretch who wanders about, who works and starves, whose life is a continual scene of sore affliction or pinching penury; can that man call England or any other kingdom his country? A country that had no bread for him, whose fields procured him no harvest, who met with nothing but the frowns of the rich, the severity of the laws, with jails and punishments; who owned not a single foot of the extensive surface of this planet?"[182]

The above statement highlights how immigrants came to America to escape injustice and poverty in Europe. Crévecoeur's choice of words to describe America as the "American asylum" is particularly interesting, as it is a country that serves as a refuge for the poor, destitute, and hopeless.

Urged by a variety of motives, here they came. Every thing has tended to regenerate them; new laws, a new mode of living, a new social system; here they are become men: in Europe they were as so many useless plants, wanting vegetative mould, and refreshing showers; they withered, and were mowed down by want, hunger, and war; but now by the

---

[181] de Crevoecoeur, J. Hector St John. *Letters from an American Farmer*. Prabhat Prakashan, 2021, pg. 25.

[182] de Crevoecoeur, J. Hector St John. *Letters from an American Farmer*. Prabhat Prakashan, 2021. pg. 19

power of transplantation, like all other plants they have taken root and flourished! Formerly they were not numbered in any civil lists of their country, except in those of the poor; here they rank as citizens. By what invisible power has this surprising metamorphosis been performed? By that of the laws and that of their industry. The laws, the indulgent laws, protect them as they arrive, stamping on them the symbol of adoption; they receive ample rewards for their labours; these accumulated rewards procure them lands; those lands confer on them the title of freemen, and to that title every benefit is affixed which men can possibly require.[183]

Crévecoeur highlights that European immigrants have left their ethnic roots behind, which is an interesting observation. He notes that these individuals, who did not have the chance to become civilized in Europe, have created a new life for themselves with laws they have created. He also draws attention to the fact that these poor farmers have become landowner capitalists by saving the rewards of their labor.

What attachment can a poor European emigrant have for a country where he had nothing? The knowledge of the language, the love of a few kindred as poor as himself, were the only cords that tied him: his country is now that which gives him land, bread, protection, and consequence: Ubi panis ibi patria, is the motto of all emigrants. What then is the American, this new man? He is either an European, or the descendant of an European, hence that strange mixture of blood, which you will find in no other country. I could point out to you a family whose grandfather was an Englishman, whose wife was Dutch, whose son married a French woman, and whose present four sons have now four wives of different nations. He is an American, who, leaving behind him all his

---

[183] de Crevoecoeur, J. Hector St John. *Letters from an American Farmer*. Prabhat Prakashan, 2021, pg. 26.

ancient prejudices and manners, receives new ones from the new mode of life he has embraced, the new government he obeys, and the new rank he holds. He becomes an American by being received in the broad lap of our great Alma Mater. Here individuals of all nations are melted into a new race of men, whose labours and posterity will one day cause great changes in the world.[184]

In the above statements, Crévecoeur describes an American as someone who comes from diverse ethnic backgrounds and embraces a new way of life, leaving behind the customs of their previous country. The primary criterion for embracing this new country is the satisfaction of the new citizen's basic needs.

Here the rewards of his industry follow with equal steps the progress of his labour; his labour is founded on the basis of nature, SELF-INTEREST: can it want a stronger allurement?

In America, individuals can receive their rewards independently, working for themselves rather than for a boss or a monarch. The capitalism that emerged in America is a form of democratic capitalism, and since everyone worked for themselves on their own farm, every immigrant initially became a small capitalist.

"Here religion demands but little of him; a small voluntary salary to the minister, and gratitude to God; can he refuse these? The American is a new man, who acts upon new principles; he must therefore entertain new ideas, and form new opinions.

---

[184] de Crevoecoeur, J. Hector St John. *Letters from an American Farmer*. Prabhat Prakashan, 2021.

An European, when he first arrives, seems limited in his intentions, as well as in his views; but he very suddenly alters his scale; two hundred miles formerly appeared a very great distance, it is now but a trifle; he no sooner breathes our air than he forms schemes, and embarks in designs he never would have thought of in his own country. There the plenitude of society confines many useful ideas, and often extinguishes the most laudable schemes which here ripen into maturity. Thus Europeans become Americans.

Crévecoeur observed that American society naturally selected good ideas before Darwin published "The Origin of Species" in 1859,[185] and he further analyzed how the pragmatic evaluation of successful projects led to their adoption. One of the United States' significant advantages is the diversity brought by people of different ethnicities melting into the American pot. Diversity provides perspectives and other inputs that can foster creativity. In his book "The Future of Management," Gary Hamel particularly notes that diversity fosters creativity in urban communities.

Diversity begets creativity. In a city, it's the diversity of cultures, perspectives, skills, industries, building styles, and neighborhoods that stoke the fires of innovation. When like meets like, there is no creative spark; but when like collides with unlike, there is often a small frisson of inspiration. If cities produce more innovation than the suburbs, it's because they are more diverse-they possess more raw material for the machinery of human imagination.

"In a city, it's the diversity of cultures, perspectives, skills, industries, building styles, and neighborhoods, that stoke the fires of innovation. When like meets with unlike, there is often a small frisson of inspiration. If cities produce more

---

[185] Charles Robert Darwin, **The Origin of Species**. Vol. XI. The Harvard Classics. New York: P.F. Collier & Son, 1909-14; Bartleby.com, 2001.

innovation than the suburbs, it's because they are more diverse-they possess more raw material for the machinery of human imagination.[186]

Although people in American society share similar values, there is cultural diversity and richness resulting from ethnic backgrounds. The convergence of these diverse elements helps to create a new and more valuable whole, like a mosaic in Turkish culture or a dish of "aşure-Noah's Pudding".

In part, great cities are able to reinvent themselves because they make it easy for individuals to reinvent themselves. Filled as they are with escapees from the stultifying conventions small town life, cities are oblivious to peculiarity. The world's creative centers are filled with self-made men and women-folks like Russell Simmons, Masatoshi Son, Donald Trump, Oprah Winfrey, Lakshmi Mittal, Steve Jobs, and Larry Ellison. In progressive cities, aptitude counts for more than provenance, and today's dropouts, misfits, and goofballs may well be tomorrow's media maven, property kingpins, and cultural icons. Cities are filled with people on the make, scrambling up and skidding down the slippery slope of fame and fortune. New arrivals quickly learn that the city's anonymity allows them to try on different value systems and pursue their eccentric passions. In cities, elastic social conventions and permeable hierarchies create space for personal growth and reinvention.[187]

Gary Hamel's reference to cities like New York, Boston, Chicago, or Los Angeles in his quote suggests that these

---

[186] Gary Hamel, Bill Breen, **The Future of Management**, Harvard Business Review Press, 2007, p.174.

[187] Gary Hamel, Bill Breen, p.174.

American cities evaluate people based on their abilities or projects rather than their origins.

As Robert Park once pointed out, small communities often reward normality and tolerate eccentricity, while cities tend to reward and encourage eccentricity.[188] In other words, a great city provides urban adventurers with the opportunity to push the limits of their own capabilities in ways that a village cannot.

The melting pot of America has rewarded adventurers and innovators who focus on their dreams and projects, rather than their roots.

3.1.9.1. Criticism to the Concept of American Melting Pot

The concept of the "melting pot" has been a central tenet of American identity for decades. It suggests that the diversity of cultures and ethnicities in the United States can be blended together to form a single, harmonious society. While this ideal has been celebrated as a source of strength and unity, it has also been subject to criticism.

One of the main criticisms of the melting pot is that it implies a homogenization of culture, where minority cultures are expected to conform to the dominant culture in order to be accepted.[189] This expectation of assimilation can lead to the erasure of unique cultural traditions and practices, as well as the marginalization of those who do not fit into the mainstream. This can create a homogenous society that

---

[188] Robert Park, E. Burgess ve R. McKenzie, **The City,** University of Chicago Press, 1925, p.41.

[189] GORDON, MILTON. "E Pluribus Unum? The myth of the melting pot." *American Studies| Volume* (2014): 257.

discourages diversity and discourages the emergence of new ideas.

Additionally, the idea of the melting pot fails to acknowledge the persistence of systemic discrimination and inequality.[190] The reality is that many minority groups face significant barriers to social and economic mobility, even when they do assimilate to mainstream culture. The melting pot ideal can also create a false sense of unity that obscures the deep-seated social and economic inequalities that exist in the United States.

Historically, the melting pot ideal has been used to justify discriminatory policies and practices. For example, in the late 19th and early 20th century, the U.S. government implemented laws that restricted immigration from certain countries in an attempt to maintain a homogenous society.[191] This exclusionary policy prevented many talented and skilled individuals from contributing to American society and stifled innovation and progress.

Moreover, the concept of the melting pot ignores the contributions of diverse cultures to American society. Many of the most important innovations and breakthroughs in the United States have been the result of cross-cultural exchange and collaboration. For example, jazz music, which is often

---

[190] Caliendo, Stephen. *Inequality in America: Race, poverty, and fulfilling democracy's promise*. Routledge, 2021.

[191] Chinese Exclusion Act (1882), An act to execute certain treaty stipulations relating to the Chinese, May 6, 1882; Enrolled Acts and Resolutions of Congress, 1789-1996; General Records of the United States Government; Record Group 11; National Archives https://www.archives.gov/milestone-documents/chinese-exclusion-act

hailed as America's only original art form,[192] was born out of a fusion of African American, European, and Latin American musical traditions.

In conclusion, while the melting pot ideal has been a central part of American identity, it is not without its flaws. The expectation of assimilation can lead to the erasure of unique cultural practices and traditions, and the ideal can create a false sense of unity that obscures the persistence of social and economic inequality. By embracing and celebrating diverse cultures, rather than forcing assimilation, it is possible to create a more inclusive and innovative society.

3.1.9.2. Concept of Melting Pot in Europe

Europe has been a historically diverse continent, with various ethnic, linguistic, and cultural groups existing side by side for centuries. However, Europe's history is marked by a complex interplay of cultural, religious, and national identities. Unlike the United States, where a significant portion of the population can trace their ancestry back to immigrants, Europe has witnessed more gradual demographic shifts and cultural evolutions over time.

In Europe, the idea of cultural assimilation has often coexisted with the preservation of distinct cultural identities. Many European countries have maintained strong ties to their cultural heritage, emphasizing the importance of language, traditions, and historical roots. This has contributed to the preservation of diverse cultural landscapes within Europe, with various communities maintaining their unique identities and customs.

That being said, Europe has experienced significant cultural and demographic transformations throughout history. Waves

---

[192] Gioia, Ted. *The history of jazz*. Oxford University Press, 2011.

of migration, colonization, and displacement have led to the mixing and blending of different cultures and ethnicities in certain regions. For example, countries like France, Germany, and the United Kingdom have witnessed the integration and acculturation of diverse immigrant populations over the years.[193] However, the degree to which these diverse cultures blend together and form a single "Melting Pot" varies across different European countries and regions.

Furthermore, Europe's approach to cultural diversity has often been shaped by a concept known as "cultural pluralism."[194] Rather than advocating for assimilation into a single dominant culture, European societies have embraced the coexistence of multiple cultural identities. This approach emphasizes mutual respect, tolerance, and recognition of diverse cultural expressions within a broader societal framework.

It is important to remember that the European continent encompasses numerous countries, each with its own unique history, culture, and approach to immigration and integration. Therefore, the presence of a "Melting Pot" phenomenon varies across different European contexts. While some European cities, such as London, Berlin, or Paris, may exhibit characteristics of cultural fusion[195] and diversity, it is more accurate to describe Europe as a mosaic of diverse cultures and identities rather than a single unified "Melting Pot."

---

[193] Delgado, Leticia. "Immigration in Europe: realities and policies." (2002).

[194] Németh, Ádám, et al. "Competing diversity índices and attitudes toward cultural pluralism in Europe." *Equality, Diversity and Inclusion: An International Journal* 41.7 (2022): 1029-1046.

[195] Croucher, Stephen M., and Eric Kramer. "Cultural fusion theory: An alternative to acculturation." *Journal of International and Intercultural Communication* 10.2 (2017): 97-114.

In conclusion, the concept of the "American Melting Pot" finds its roots in the unique historical and social context of the United States, shaped by centuries of immigration and cultural assimilation. While Europe has a rich tapestry of diverse cultures and ethnicities, its historical and cultural dynamics have fostered a different approach to cultural identity and assimilation. Europe's diverse cultural landscapes, historical roots, and emphasis on cultural pluralism contribute to a more nuanced understanding of cultural diversity on the continent, distinct from the notion of a singular "Melting Pot" seen in the United States.

People don't understand that when I grew up, I was never the most talented. I was never the biggest. I was never the fastest. I certainly was never the strongest. The only thing I had was my work ethic, and that's been what has gotten me this far.
Tiger Woods

3.1.10. Protestant Work Ethic

The Protestant Work Ethic is a prominent aspect of the American mindset, along with capitalist ideals. The pursuit of efficiency in capitalism and the focus on work in the Protestant Work Ethic have set Americans apart from other cultures in terms of their work ethic. Max Weber argued in his book, "The Protestant Ethic and the Spirit of Capitalism,"[196] that Puritanism and its ideas influenced the development of capitalism. Weber's book was not a detailed study of the Protestant denomination, but rather an analysis of the interaction between religion and economy. While religious devotion usually involves rejecting worldly goals, in Protestantism, the pursuit of wealth and prosperity is also present. Weber addresses this dilemma in his book.

Weber emphasizes that capitalists originated from the Protestant community, not just in Europe, but also in other countries. Capitalists and employers, as well as the educated upper class of workers in modern industries with high technical or commercial education, all possess Protestant characteristics. Weber notes that people who practice Protestantism are mainly found in economically developed regions where production is high. The fact that Protestants make up a large proportion of the population in terms of capital can be attributed, in part, to historical roots. This context stretches far back into the past, and being a member of a particular denomination is seen as a result, rather than a cause, of economic appearances. Participating in the aforementioned economic functions sometimes involves owning capital, having an expensive education, or both. Today, these factors are tied to inherited wealth. The majority of the wealthiest people, particularly those in the richest cities with the most favorable natural resources and social

---

[196] Weber, Max. *The Protestant work ethic and the spirit of capitalism.* Allen and Unwin, 1976.

networks, adopted Protestantism in the 16th century, and its effects continue to support the economic struggles of Protestants.

Weber makes sharp distinctions between Catholics and Protestants within Christianity. According to Weber, Catholic doctrine tends to keep a Catholic in a certain level of mastery in the business world, while a Protestant desires to move from skilled labor to management. Weber claims that Catholics are more peaceful, less motivated to earn, and prefer even a little income to the dangerous lifestyle that can bring honor and wealth in the end. The proverb is jokingly saying either eat well or sleep well. Protestants, on the other hand, want to eat very well.

Before delving into connections with religion, Weber attempts to define the spirit of capitalism in order to explain it. He supports his definition with a quote from Benjamin Franklin.

> *Remember, that time is money. He that can earn ten shillings a day by his labour, and goes abroad, or sits idle, one half of that day, though he spends but sixpence during his diversion or idleness, ought not to reckon that the only expense; he has really spent, or rather thrown away, five shillings besides. Remember, that credit is money. If a man lets his money lie in my hands after it is due, he gives me the interest, or so much the protestant ethic and the spirit of capitalism as I can make of it during that time. This amounts to a considerable sum where a man has good and large credit, and makes good use of it. Remember, that money is of the prolific, generating nature.*
> *Money can beget money, and its offspring can beget more, and so on. Five shillings turned is six, turned again it is seven and threepence, and so on, till it becomes a hundred pounds. The more there is of it, the more it produces every turning, so that the profits rise quicker and quicker. He that kills a breedingsow,destroys all her offspring to the*

thousandth generation. He that murders a crown, destroys all that it might have produced, even scores of pounds.[197]

Weber explains the "spirit of capitalism" by quoting Benjamin Franklin: The capitalist works constantly without wasting any leisure time, acquires money to profit from its time value or interest, and reinvests the money to earn more. Max Weber also elucidates other features of the "spirit of capitalism" by citing quotes from Franklin.

> *Remember this saying, The good paymaster is lord of anotherman's purse. He that is known to pay punctually and exactly to the time he promises, may at any time, and on any occasion, raise all the money his friends can spare. This is sometimes of great use. After industry and frugality, nothing contributes more to the raising of a young man in the world than punctuality and justice in all his dealings; therefore never keep borrowed money an hour beyond the time you promised, lest a disappointment shut up your friend's purse for ever.*

With this statement, Benjamin Franklin highlights the fundamental concepts of "trust" and "reliability" in business life. It is related to branding and recognition in all fields, and keeping one's promises.

> The most trifling actions that affect a man's credit are to be regarded. The sound of your hammer at five in the morning, or eight at night, heard by a creditor, makes him easy six months longer; but if he sees you at a billiard-table, or hears your voice at a tavern, when you should be at work, he sends for his money the next day; demands it, before he can receive it, in a lump.

---

[197] Franklin, Benjamin. "Advice to a Young Tradesman, (21 July 1748)". Founders Online. National Archives and Records Administration/University of Virginia Press. Archived from the original on August 23, 2019. Retrieved November 1, 2019.

Benjamin Franklin emphasizes the importance of both continuous hard work and waking up early with this statement. According to Weber, the Spirit of Capitalism is crystallized in Benjamin Franklin's words. Weber argues that all of Franklin's moral approaches have turned into utilitarianism: "Honesty is useful, because it assures credit; so are punctuality, industry, frugality, and that is the reason they are virtues."

Weber believes that Franklin is more deeply committed to virtues than is apparent in this statement. According to Weber's analysis, the Spirit of Capitalism reflects the following idea: "Man is dominated by the making of money, by acquisition as the ultimate purpose of his life. Economic acquisition is no longer subordinated to man as the means for the satisfaction of his material needs."

Weber thinks that Franklin's approach also includes a series of emotions that closely express religious concepts. "If we thus ask, why should 'money be made out of men,' Benjamin Franklin himself, although he was a colorless deist, answers in his autobiography with a quotation from the Bible, which his strict Calvinistic father drummed into him again and again in his youth: 'Seest thou a man diligent in his business? He shall stand before kings' (Prov. xxii. 29). The earning of money within the modern economic order is, so long as it is done legally, the result and the expression of virtue and proficiency in a calling." Based on this, Weber emphasizes that in the spirit of capitalism, work itself, rather than money, is the reward for specialization and determination.

According to Weber, capitalism forces individuals to conform to the rules of commercial relationships as long as they are engaged in exchange relationships. Workers who cannot conform or do not want to conform to these rules are thrown out of work just as factory owners who take actions against these rules are pushed out of economic life. Today's capitalism that governs economic life educates and selects economic agents-employers and workers-based on their economic resilience. Weber emphasizes that the selection of a lifestyle and profession that matches the characteristics of capitalism requires the adoption of its rules and understanding by a group of people.

Weber analyzes the relationship between the Spirit of Capitalism and ascetic Protestantism by first defining ascetic Protestantism. According to Weber, asceticism is a view that seeks the salvation of the soul from a religious perspective by devoting oneself to divine purposes by staying away from worldly pleasures. Weber states that there are four branches of ascetic Protestantism: Calvinism, Pietism, Methodism, and Baptism. According to Weber, these movements are not entirely separate from each other and are not opposed to each other.

To examine the relationship between the fundamental religious concepts of ascetic Protestantism and the principles of action in daily economic life, it is necessary to refer first and foremost to the theological writings arising from the practices of the salvation of the soul. Weber attempts to approach ascetic Protestantism as a whole in his book. Since English Puritanism, which emerged from Calvinism, provides the most consistent foundation for the concept of vocation, Weber places one of its representatives at the center of the discussion. He chooses Richard Baxter, the most popular writer on Puritan ethics, and continues his analysis with reference to him.

For Protestants, according to Weber, the path to reward in the afterlife is through working in the service of God. However, this is not traditional worship in the usual sense, but rather the practice of one's profession.

According to Max Weber, wasting time is the first and deadliest sin, as human life is infinitely short and precious to ensure one's own salvation. Time lost through socializing, idle talk, luxury, or even more sleep than necessary for health (six to eight hours) is morally condemned. While Weber doesn't fully agree with Franklin's idea that time is money, he does believe it holds true in a spiritual sense. Every hour lost is an hour not spent working for the glory of God. Thus, inactive contemplation is considered valueless or even reprehensible if it interferes with daily work. In God's eyes, active performance of His will in a calling is more pleasing than inactive contemplation.

Work is, above all, the purpose of life as written by God himself. St. Paul's statement "he who does not work, shall not eat" applies to everyone. A reluctance to work is a sign of the lack of consecration.

Working is not just for the poor or middle-class people to become rich; it is for everyone. Working and practicing a profession is a commandment given to all. Even if the wealthy do not need to work to buy something, they should still work because it is a divine commandment.

> Even the wealthy shall not eat without working, for even though they do not need to labour to support their own needs, there is God's commandment which they, like the poor, must obey. For everyone without exception God's Providence has prepared a calling, which he should profess and in which he should labour. And this calling is not, as it was for the Lutheran,30 a fate to which he must submit and which he must make the best of, but God's commandment to the individual to work for the divine glory.[198]

---

[198] Weber, Max. *The Protestant work ethic and the spirit of capitalism*. Allen and Unwin, 1976.

Surprisingly, Puritanism also emphasized vocational productivity. The highest productivity is achieved through specialization in one's profession. Within the Puritan perspective, the divine nature of mutual economic gain takes on a different appearance. The divine purpose of division of labor is recognized from the pragmatic interpretation of Puritan tendency. Baxter's explanations, in several respects, recall Adam Smith's praise of division of labor. Specialization in a profession leads to an increase in both quantitative and qualitative production, as it enables the worker's ability to improve, and it serves the common good, which is the maximum possible number of goods. So far, the driving force is simply a creative drive.

According to Weber, Baxter puts the original Puritan quest for productivity at the forefront of his discussion. The moral conformity of a profession that pleases God is first measured according to moral rules, and then towards the importance of goods produced for the common good. However, at that point, the third and, naturally, the most important practical point of view emerges: private economic profitability.

For if that God who affects the life of the producer at every formation gives a chance of winning to someone who is like Him, He does so for a purpose. And the faithful Christian responds to this call that will benefit him. "If God shows you a way of legally earning more than you would by any other means, without harming yourself, someone else, or His Spirit, and you refuse it, and follow a less profitable path, you violate one of the purposes of your profession; you refuse to be God's representative and reject His gifts, which He has given you and which you can use for Him when He wants."

According to Protestant asceticism, people do not work just to become rich or to satisfy their carnal pleasures. However, if people work tirelessly and do not consume what they earn, capital accumulation occurs:

To become rich, one must work for God, not for bodily pleasures and sin. If wealth is a stimulus against laziness and sinful pleasures of life, it is then dangerous, and if it is pursued in order to live carefree and comfortably, it is only bad. Considering the limitation of consumption in tandem with the pursuit of gain, the practical outcome is lucid: the savings derived from asceticism result in accumulated capital.

According to Weber, the obstacles to the consumption of earned income have contributed to the productive use of capital. In other words, the earnings were not spent but rather saved, resulting in the growth of capital. The strength of this effect cannot be precisely determined by numbers. In Holland, which was governed by strict Calvinism for seven years, the simple lifestyle prevalent among the most devout religious communities combined with great wealth to result in excessive capital accumulation.

As evident from the above quotes, constant work is fundamental to capitalism, as emphasized by Benjamin Franklin's statements. Investing earned money and growing it in various ways are also core tenets of capitalism. However, even though it has a functional side, one cannot be a good capitalist without being a moral and honest person.

On the other hand, Protestant asceticism calls for people to work for the afterlife and save rather than spend. It is believed that those who work hard, become wealthy, and do not waste their wealth will go to heaven. These teachings are emphasized directly or indirectly in the fundamental texts taught in churches. A Protestant American raised with these doctrines will think in this way and strive to live according to these teachings. The hardworking and productivity-oriented nature of Americans throughout history is no coincidence.

3.1.10.1 Criticism to Protestant Work Ethic

Criticism of the Protestant Work Ethic[199] in the United States stems from various perspectives that question its influence on entrepreneurship and innovation. While the Protestant Work Ethic is often lauded for its emphasis on hard work, discipline, and individual responsibility, it is important to critically examine its potential negative effects.

One criticism is that the Protestant Work Ethic can lead to an excessive focus on work and material success at the expense of other aspects of life. The relentless pursuit of productivity and financial gain may lead individuals to prioritize work over personal relationships, leisure time, and overall well-being.[200] This can create an imbalance in life, potentially resulting in burnout, stress-related health issues, and strained social connections.

Additionally, the emphasis on individual effort and success can undermine the recognition of systemic barriers and inequalities that may impede entrepreneurship and innovation. The Protestant Work Ethic tends to attribute success solely to individual qualities, such as hard work and moral virtue,[201] while overlooking the role of privilege, access to resources, and social networks in shaping opportunities. This perspective can perpetuate the myth of meritocracy and disregard the structural factors that impact entrepreneurship, particularly for marginalized communities.

---

[199] Crowell, Ethan. *Weber's "Protestant ethic" and his critics*. The University of Texas at Arlington, 2006.

[200] Spence, Janet T. "Achievement American style: The rewards and costs of individualism." *American Psychologist* 40.12 (1985): 1285.

[201] Mudrack, Peter E. "Protestant work-ethic dimensions and work orientations." *Personality and individual differences* 23.2 (1997): 217-225.

Moreover, the Protestant Work Ethic's focus on earthly achievements and material wealth may limit the pursuit of innovative and socially impactful ventures. Innovation often requires risk-taking, experimentation, and the willingness to challenge existing norms and structures. The pressure to conform to societal expectations of success and the pursuit of financial gain may stifle entrepreneurial creativity and discourage ventures that prioritize social or environmental goals over immediate profitability.

Furthermore, the Protestant Work Ethic's association of prosperity with moral righteousness can lead to a judgmental and exclusionary mindset. This can create a culture that places undue pressure[202] on individuals to conform to societal expectations and stigmatizes those who may not fit the mold of the "successful entrepreneur." Such an environment can discourage diversity, limit inclusivity, and hinder the emergence of new perspectives and innovative ideas.

In conclusion, while the Protestant Work Ethic has been credited with fostering a strong work ethic and personal responsibility, it is crucial to critically evaluate its potential negative effects on entrepreneurship and innovation. By promoting an excessive focus on work, overlooking structural barriers, and prioritizing material success over holistic well-being and societal impact, the Protestant Work Ethic may inadvertently hinder the cultivation of a truly inclusive and innovative entrepreneurial ecosystem. Recognizing the limitations of this ethic can pave the way for a more balanced and inclusive approach to entrepreneurship and innovation that considers broader societal well-being and systemic factors.

---

[202] Porter, Gayle. "Work, work ethic, work excess." *Journal of organizational change management* 17.5 (2004): 424-439.

3.1.10.2 Religious Work Ethic in Europe

Both America and Continental Europe have been positively impacted by the Protestant Work Ethic in terms of entrepreneurship, innovation, and economic growth, although the extent and manifestation of its influence may vary between the two regions.

In America, the Protestant Work Ethic played a crucial role in shaping the cultural and economic landscape. The early settlers, predominantly of Protestant faith, brought with them a strong emphasis on hard work, personal responsibility, and the pursuit of economic prosperity. This mindset fostered a climate conducive to entrepreneurship and innovation, as individuals sought to realize their ambitions through industriousness and dedication. The Protestant belief in the dignity of labor and the idea that one's work was a calling from God fueled the entrepreneurial spirit, leading to the establishment of numerous successful businesses and industries.

America's history as a nation of immigrants further contributed to the influence of the Protestant Work Ethic. People from diverse backgrounds arrived in the United States with dreams of economic advancement and embraced the values of hard work, self-reliance, and upward mobility. This blending of cultures and aspirations created a fertile ground for entrepreneurship and innovation to flourish.

In Continental Europe, the impact of the Protestant Work Ethic on entrepreneurship, innovation, and economic growth is also significant, albeit with some variations. Countries with a strong Protestant tradition, such as Germany[203], the Netherlands, and Switzerland, have experienced notable economic success and industrialization. The emphasis on hard

---

[203] Spenkuch, Jörg L. "The Protestant Ethic and work: Micro evidence from contemporary Germany." (2011).

work, discipline, and personal responsibility in these societies contributed to their capacity for innovation, scientific advancements, and the establishment of thriving business enterprises.

However, it is important to point that Continental Europe's economic growth and innovation cannot be solely attributed to the Protestant Work Ethic. Other factors, such as geographic location, natural resources, historical context, political structures, and educational systems, have also played significant roles. Additionally, different regions within Continental Europe have their own cultural, religious, and historical influences that shape their approach to entrepreneurship and economic development.

Furthermore, it is essential to acknowledge that other European countries with different religious and cultural traditions have also experienced remarkable economic growth and innovation.[204] For example, countries like France, Italy, and Spain, with predominantly Catholic populations, have made significant contributions to various fields of entrepreneurship and innovation throughout history.

Overall, while the Protestant Work Ethic has influenced both America and Continental Europe in fostering an entrepreneurial spirit, innovation, and economic growth, it is important to recognize that multiple factors contribute to the success of these regions. Cultural, historical, and socioeconomic contexts, along with other institutional and systemic factors, play pivotal roles in shaping the entrepreneurial ecosystems and economic dynamics of each region.

---

[204] Nelson, Robert H. "Is Max Weber Newly Relevant?: The Protestant-Catholic Divide in Europe Today." *Finnish Journal of Theology* 5 (2012).

Idealism loses to pragmatism when it comes to winning elections.
Danny Strong

3.1.11. Pragmatism

Pragmatism is a philosophical movement that emerged and developed in American thought, with a significant impact on American life.[205] In other words, Americans did not become pragmatists by learning about Pragmatism; they became pragmatists by living this philosophy without necessarily naming it. The articulation and dissemination of this philosophy in American life have contributed to the widespread acceptance and development of pragmatism.

Pragmatism is a philosophy that originated and flourished in the second half of the 19th century in America. It is a practical philosophy that aims to apply people's ideas, beliefs, or knowledge to human life, to make them useful and to contribute to the resolution of various problems encountered in different fields.

At the heart of Pragmatism lies the following approach: If a philosophy is to be formulated, it must be structured in a method that can guide people not only through intellectual difficulties but also through the resolution of all practical problems encountered in everyday life. Thus, pragmatism is less a philosophy that involves abstract ideas than a thinking method that has active results. It can be defined as "a philosophical approach that places practical activities at the center, and considers the expected results/benefits in practical activities to be the primary purpose of human effort."

Pragmatism is a principle of inquiry and an account of meaning first proposed by C. S. Peirce in the 1870s. The crux of Peirce's pragmatism is that for any statement to be meaningful, it must have practical bearings. Peirce saw the

---

[205] Bacon, Michael. *Pragmatism: an introduction*. Polity, 2012.

pragmatic account of meaning as a method for clearing up metaphysics and aiding scientific inquiry.[206]

Pragmatism is empirical, science-based, utilitarian, and based on observable data. In Pragmatism, the meanings of ideas and concepts are not static but determined by the visible effects and results associated with them. Consequently, knowledge and truth are not absolute but relative to the stage of observation. From a pragmatist perspective, a scientific truth is a thought that is useful in practice and can solve a problem. As William James said, "Truth is what works in our way of thinking. Good is what works in our way of behaving." The concept of usefulness is central to pragmatism. In other words, any knowledge that works in practice is true and good. Its truthfulness depends on its compatibility with the way of thinking, and its goodness depends on its compatibility with the way of behavior.

Pragmatism as a philosophical movement has led to numerous reforms in various areas of American society. In the American education system, practical knowledge and behavior models that can be applied and demonstrate their value and usefulness in practice have taken precedence over institutional and abstract knowledge and lessons. The emphasis on subjects such as business management and engineering in the American education system can be seen as a result of Pragmatism. The image of an individual who produces results, solves problems, creates value through work, achieves successful outcomes, is enterprising, self-confident, and individualistic is a direct result of Pragmatism.

Pragmatism promotes the advocacy of practical, problem-solving ideas or knowledge that is applicable and useful, and thus places the concept of "utility" at the center of its

---

[206] Charles Sanders Peirce: Pragmatism, https://iep.utm.edu/peircepr, Retrieved on September, 20, 2023.

philosophy. While its utilitarian approach may make Pragmatism appear to be a simple philosophy, on the other hand, its empirical foundation, which is based on observation and experimentation, makes it a philosophy that is rooted in science and its methods.

Pragmatism has contributed to many areas of philosophy, including empiricism, positivism, philosophy of science, methodology, and theories of meaning. In Pragmatism, there are no absolute truths; rather, the correctness of a thought or belief depends on its consistency and usefulness. This approach does not idealize concepts, but instead, it creates a valid truth for every context based on its practical implications, regardless of geography, time, or subjective circumstances. Pragmatism also simplifies concepts by avoiding the use of unhelpful concepts and phenomena.

The concept of "utility" in Pragmatism is sometimes associated with the concept of "interest." However, utility and interest are distinct concepts in Pragmatism. The basic principle of utility is usefulness, while interest does not always have to result in usefulness. For instance, circulating hot water through radiators on a cold winter day is useful, whereas using the same water to sell coal at four times the market price is an example of an interest-seeking endeavor. Although a particular interest may provide some benefit to a person, not every benefit necessarily has to be regarded as an interest.

In this study, a definition of "Pragmatism" can be presented, but care is taken not to provide definitive answers when trying to explain the specific conditions of the American context. In America, there is no single definition of "pragmatism" that all authors agree on. Different authors and thinkers have different interpretations and applications of the concept.

The main founders of Pragmatism are generally considered to be Charles Sanders Peirce, Henry James, and John Dewey. Charles Sander Peirce (1839-1914), who is the founder and namesake of Pragmatism,[207] proposes that Pragmatism is a method for illuminating the meanings of concepts that are abstract, fuzzy, or uncertain. He established the "pragmatic maxim," which states that concepts with unclear meanings can be replaced with concepts that have clear meanings. However, this replacement is performed within an operation or process, within the context of conditional proposition templates. The meaning referred to is not initially a clear meaning, but it is a meaning that emerges as a result of a specific process or continues until the operational meaning is made clear. In this way, it gains real sensory, factual, objective clarity, and pragmatic clarity. "Let us consider the effects that can be produced by the concept we entertain. Then our conception of these effects is the whole of our conception of the object." From Peirce's thought, it can concluded that metaphysics and abstract concepts cannot be subjected to an operational process, and therefore their real meanings cannot be obtained. According to Peirce, ideal knowledge is knowledge that solves natural and human difficulties. Truth is not an abstract thing, but a concrete thing that can demonstrate its effects.

After Charles Sanders Peirce, William James (1842-1910) is accepted as the second leader of Pragmatism.[208] Like Peirce, James links truth to factual reality in a finite sense. In other words, he links the truth of something to its consequences. Truth is not a fixed quality of thought or belief. A belief that works in practice, by virtue of its usefulness, proves to be true.

---

[207] Pragmatism, Stanford Encyclopedia of Philosophy, https://plato.stanford.edu/index.html, retrieved on September 21, 2023.

[208] Philip P. Wiener, **Evolution and the Founders of Pragmatism**, Peter Smith Pub., 1969.

If a previously successful belief no longer works or solves our problem, it has become false information. In short, beliefs and ideas are verified or falsified depending on the conditions. An idea becomes true when it starts working, and as long as it works, it retains its truth. Therefore, truth is not an absolute thing, but a consequence of its usefulness.

James explained pragmatism in a more understandable language in an interview with the New York Times in 1907. He stated, "Actually, most of our thinking is for the purpose of prompting actions that will help us change the world, and the criteria of true thought should be its efficacy in this regard. Theoretical accuracy comes after practical application. Theoretical accuracy is based on the previous efficacy of practical application, and so the chain continues such that every accuracy that involves human practice has a foundation. Thus, with a good conscience, we are free to use both our theoretical and practical abilities to make the world a better place." [209]

"Dewey's pragmatism — or, "cultural naturalism", which he favored over "pragmatism" and "instrumentalism" — may be understood as a critique and reconstruction of philosophy within the larger ambit of a Darwinian worldview. Following James' lead, Dewey argued that philosophy had become an overly technical and intellectualistic discipline, divorced from assessing the social conditions and values dominating everyday life. He sought to reconnect philosophy with the mission of education-for-living (philosophy as "the general

---

[209] PRAGMATISM --- WHAT IT IS --- BY PROF WILLIAM JAMES; Harvard Philosopher Explains that His Stand Is Entirely for "a Philosophy That Works" and a Man Who Shapes His Own Fate. A Skepticism Which Sees the Impossibility to the Human Mind of Attaining Real Truth, So Studies the Laws of Phenomena. *New York Times Interview*, published on November 3, 1907, https://www.nytimes.com/1907/11/03/archives/pragmatism-what-it-is-by-prof-william-james-harvard-philosopher.html?searchResultPosition=19

theory of education"), a form of social criticism at the most general level, or criticism of criticisms."[210]

Dewey defines claiming that a belief or knowledge is true as declaring it to be reliable and that it will remain so in every perceptible circumstance. Dewey's pragmatism has a more universal quality. For example, from the perspective of the United States, invading Iraq is the right thing to do because it leads to the seizure of oil. However, this interpretation of pragmatism is incorrect according to Dewey's approach. In Dewey's pursuit of a universal truth, the right thing should be true in every perceptible circumstance. In the case of Iraq, invading another country cannot be right in every perceptible circumstance.

Dewey believes that philosophy's primary task is to find a serious and rational solution to the divisive and harmful separation between science and values. The problem of restoring unity and cooperation between beliefs about the world in which humans live and beliefs about values and purposes that govern human behavior is the most significant problem of modern life.

It is evident that Dewey emphasizes values, striving for consistency and coherence among them; in this regard, he distinguishes himself from other pragmatists.

In America, the form of governance, including laws and inventions, is judged by its outcomes, and a lasting form is established through a kind of Darwinian natural selection. Numerous options are put into practice, and those that prove successful become permanent. Therefore, more important than ideas themselves are their applications, since the goodness or badness of an idea is only understood through its

---

[210]   John   Dewey,   Stanford   Encyclopedia   of   Philosophy,
https://plato.stanford.edu/entries/dewey/, retrieved on September 21, 2023.

application. In the context of American entrepreneurship, entrepreneurs consistently strive to implement a wide array of ideas.

3.1.11.1 Criticism to American Pragmatism

American pragmatism, which values practicality and usefulness above all else, has played a significant role in the success of American entrepreneurship. However, there are also criticisms of this approach, particularly when it comes to the long-term impact on society and the environment.

One criticism of pragmatism in entrepreneurship is that it can lead to a focus on short-term gains rather than sustainable, long-term growth.[211] For example, companies may prioritize profits over environmental concerns, leading to negative impacts on the planet and future generations.

Another criticism is that pragmatism can lead to a lack of moral responsibility. In the quest for practical solutions, ethical considerations may be ignored, leading to unethical or even illegal behavior. The focus on results and outcomes can also result in a culture of hyper-competition, where companies prioritize winning at all costs over ethical behavior.

Historically, the pragmatism of American entrepreneurship can be seen in the growth of industries such as oil and gas, which have prioritized profits over environmental concerns. The Exxon Valdez oil spill[212] in 1989 is one example of the negative consequences of this short-term thinking. In the tech industry, the move-fast-and-break-things mentality of Silicon Valley has resulted in numerous ethical concerns around data

---

[211] Simpson, Barbara. "Pragmatism: A philosophy of practice." *The SAGE handbook of qualitative business and management research methods* (2018): 54-68.

[212] Paine, Robert T., et al. "Trouble on oiled waters: lessons from the Exxon Valdez oil spill." *Annual Review of Ecology and Systematics* 27.1 (1996): 197-235.

privacy, social responsibility, and the impact on society as a whole.

However, there are also examples of pragmatism leading to positive change. Henry Ford's use of assembly line production revolutionized the automobile industry and made cars accessible to the masses.[213] Ford's pragmatism also led to his decision to double his workers' wages, creating a stable and loyal workforce that helped his company succeed.

In conclusion, while American pragmatism has played a significant role in the success of entrepreneurship in the United States, there are also valid criticisms of this approach. The focus on practicality and outcomes can sometimes lead to short-term thinking and a lack of ethical consideration. However, with thoughtful consideration of long-term consequences and a commitment to ethical behavior, pragmatism can lead to positive and sustainable change.

3.1.11.2. The Dominant Philosophy and its effects on Entrepreneurship in Europe

Between the 17th century and now, Europe has not had a dominant philosophy equivalent to Pragmatism that emerged in the United States. Pragmatism is a philosophical approach that emphasizes practicality, problem-solving, and the importance of outcomes and results. It promotes the idea that ideas and beliefs should be tested and evaluated based on their practical implications and effectiveness.

In Europe, various philosophical traditions have shaped the intellectual landscape, including rationalism, empiricism, existentialism, and idealism. These philosophical movements have focused on different aspects of knowledge, truth, and

---

[213] Nye, David E. *America's assembly line*. MIT Press, 2013.

human existence, but they have not coalesced into a unified pragmatic philosophy as seen in the United States.

The absence of a dominant pragmatic philosophy in Europe does not mean that European societies lack a pragmatic mindset or a focus on practicality. Many European countries have a long history of pragmatism in their approach to governance, economics, and problem-solving. However, these pragmatic tendencies are often influenced by a range of factors, including cultural, historical, and institutional contexts specific to each country.

When it comes to entrepreneurship and innovation, Europe has witnessed significant contributions and achievements. European countries have a rich history of innovation, scientific discoveries, and technological advancements. The entrepreneurial spirit is prevalent in many European societies, with numerous successful businesses and startups emerging across various industries.

The European approach to entrepreneurship and innovation often encompasses a blend of factors, including economic policies, educational systems, cultural diversity, and collaboration between academia and industry. European countries have also established supportive frameworks for research and development, intellectual property protection, and venture capital funding.

While the United States is often associated with a more explicit focus on pragmatism and outcomes-driven thinking, Europe's approach to entrepreneurship and innovation is characterized by a combination of pragmatism, cultural diversity, historical context, and local variations. European countries often prioritize sustainability, social responsibility, and long-term planning alongside economic considerations, which can shape their approach to entrepreneurship and innovation.

In conclusion, while Europe does not have a dominant philosophy equivalent to Pragmatism as seen in the United States, it has fostered an environment that encourages entrepreneurship and innovation through a combination of factors. The European approach draws on cultural diversity, historical context, and a range of philosophical traditions, alongside pragmatic considerations, to drive economic growth, technological advancements, and societal progress.

Ultimately, permanent lunar bases will have to be anchored to permanent commercial facilities. Without property rights there will be no justification for investment and the risk to life.
Robert Bigelow

3.1.12. *Property Rights*

Entrepreneurship, being a movement towards increasing personal wealth, can more easily flourish in a society with private property rights. The United States has been a country that has revered private property rights since its founding.[214] In fact, one could say that the pursuit of private property rights was the very reason for America's establishment. Immigrants who did not want to accept the remote control of Royal England on their lands fought to establish a Republic in order to gain control over their lands.

The conceptual foundations of private property were laid down by John Locke. In his work "Two Treatises of Government,"[215] Locke stated that property "in general" was people's "lives, liberties, and estates." As can be seen, according to Locke's philosophy, life, liberty, and property are an inseparable whole and are generally explained by the concept of property.

Locke believed that property rights were acquired through labor. He stated that God had given the earth to humans to share equally. Humans work the world, produce, and whatever they take from nature through their labor belongs to them. The real source of property is human labor and effort, and there is no role for any contract, law, or authority in acquiring property other than working.

Locke argued that humans had a natural right to things they put their labor into, such as the land they enclosed and tilled. Private property came about because humans extended their personality to the produced object by exerting their energy on

---

[214] Banner, Stuart. *American property: A history of how, why, and what we own.* Harvard University Press, 2011.

[215] Johne Locke, **Two Treaties of Goverment**, Cambridge University Press, 1988, s.184.

it. Humans, by spending their own power on the product, made them their own property. Their usefulness is generally proportional to the amount of labor expended on them.

In America, people have tried to develop themselves through their labor, as a result of this understanding of private property. In America, there is more freedom in terms of how owned land can be used compared to Europe. In Europe, even if you own land, the government decides whether you can farm it or build on it.[216] Of course, there are also regulations in America, but the rules generally prioritize protecting an individual's property rights.

Since its inception, the presence of property rights in America has also made it possible for entrepreneurship to thrive. Americans, as a legal society, have not only complied with rules on all matters of rights but have also protected private property rights. The emergence of entrepreneurship is, of course, dependent on the ability to preserve wealth that results from entrepreneurship. The existence of private property rights, both philosophically and legally, has been the foundation of capitalist and entrepreneurial life in America.

In America, the sanctity of private property has made it easier for individuals to accumulate wealth by turning their hard-earned income into savings. In countries governed by monarchies, dictatorships, or communist regimes, the government's control over individuals' wealth renders working to become wealthy meaningless. Similarly, for acquired wealth to remain in the country, the owners of that wealth must feel safe and secure with their property.

---

[216] Thom McEvoy, Private Property Rights, A Look at Its History and Future, Fruit Notes, Volume 66, 2001, http://www.umas.edu/fruitadvisor/fruitnotes/privatepropertyrights.pdf., (20.08.2011).

The American Dream, frequently synonymous with prosperity and success, is predominantly characterized by the attainment of wealth. It is a concept embraced by a myriad of individuals, including renowned artists, software developers, industrialists, and proprietors of restaurant chains, who have aspired to or have achieved affluence through their respective creations and endeavors. Safeguarding this acquired wealth is integral, serving as the linchpin in upholding the essence and viability of the American Dream. The continuous pursuit of this dream reinforces the diverse tapestry of ambitions and aspirations that define the nation's core values and principles. Likewise, the concept of the American melting pot would not be possible without property rights. There would be no reason to immigrate to an America without property rights and forget one's national identity. Without property rights, there can be no talk of equal opportunities because if property rights are not protected, someone else can forcibly take that property and disturb equality.

In addition to property rights, one of America's most distinguishing and prominent features is intellectual and industrial property rights.[217] Intellectual property rights cover creative works such as software, music, lyrics, books, and industrial property rights involve patents and licenses related to industry.

In America, a patent grants the original inventor a 20-year monopoly right to the product.[218] No one else can use the same technique to produce the product except the patent

---

[217] Wilf, Steven. "Intellectual Property." *A Companion to American Legal History* (2013): 441-459.

[218] Frequently Asked Questions: Patents, World Intellectual Property Organization, https://www.wipo.int/patents/en/faq_patents.html, retrieved on September 20, 2023.

holder.[219] This allows the patent holder to turn their idea into production and become wealthy through that production. Patent protection makes dealing with inventions more reasonable. If intellectual property can be protected, it is valuable and people can aim to become wealthy by making discoveries.

During the 13 Colonies period, inventors in America could obtain patents to sell their inventions. The Patent and Copyright Clause was proposed by James Madison and Charles Cotesworth Pinckney in 1787, and was included in the US Constitution.[220]

The founders of the United States, who prepared and signed the first American Constitution, created a set of rules that guaranteed entrepreneurship in America. Particularly, the eighth section of the American Constitution secured potential entrepreneurship and trade in the country by regulating various aspects such as taxation, interstate commerce, postal system, patent and copyright laws, money printing, import and export tariffs, weight and measurement systems, performance of contracts, bankruptcy and protection of businesses. It is a fact that these regulations have had a significant impact on America's development. In particular, the implementation of patent and copyright laws, with the founding of the country, legally secured innovation and invention in the US. The eighth section of the Constitution

---

[219] Thomas Terrell, **The law and practice relating to letters patent for inventions**, Forgotten Books, 2012, s.176-178.

[220] Thomas H. Cox, Gibbons ve Ogden, **Law, and Society in the Early Republic**, Ohio University Press, 2009, s.10.

protected the works and inventions of writers and inventors, allowing patents or books to be sold as private property.[221]

The first patent law passed from the American Congress was on April 10, 1790. According to this law, a working model of the invention had to be submitted with the patent application. In 1793, a change was made to the law that simplified the patent application process. A written description of the invention was sufficient for the patent application. The office that accepted the application could request additional information if needed.[222]

The level of patent rights development is a key determinant of a country's innovation landscape. Countries like England, Italy, France, and the United States have significantly fostered innovation by establishing robust patent systems. These systems enable the easy buying and selling of inventions and provide inventors with temporary monopolies, incentivizing groundbreaking discoveries.
On the contrary, when eyes are returned to Eastern Europe, specifically the Ottoman Empire, a different historical context can be observed. In this region, the first significant copyright legislation, the Copyright Regulation of 1857, was introduced, with the Copyright and Translation Regulation following in 1870 to complete the framework.[223] In contrast, the United States, with its roots in British history, had patent and

---

[221] The Constitution for the United States, http://www.earlyamerica.com/earlyamerica/freedom/constitution/text.html, (20.08.2011).

[222] Walterscheid, Edward C. "The early evolution of the United States patent law: Antecedents (Part 1)." *J. Pat. & Trademark Off. Soc'y* 76 (1994): 697.

[223] Diren Çakmak, Osmanlı Telif Hukuku ile İlgili Mevzuat, **Türkiyat Araştırmaları Dergisi**, sayı: 21. http://www.turkiyat.selcuk.edu.tr/pdfdergi/s21/cakmak.pdf, (20.08.2011). Diren Çakmak, Osmanlı Telif Hukuku ile İlgili Mevzuat, Türkiyat Araştırmaları Dergisi, sayı: 21. http://www.turkiyat.selcuk.edu.tr/pdfdergi/s21/cakmak.pdf, (20.08.2011).

copyright laws in place even before its founding in 1796. This historical disparity partially elucidates the disparity in innovation between the Ottoman Empire and Turkey, on one hand, and the United States on the other.

In America, intellectual property rights can be seen as the backbone of entrepreneurship throughout the country. From the East Coast to the West Coast, scientists, businesspeople, and all types of researchers who strive to make new inventions are able to continue their work by being able to protect the intellectual property rights of their inventions and sell them. Without intellectual property rights, it would be impossible to imagine the existence of companies such as Facebook, Microsoft, WhatsApp, Google, Apple, GE, or Boeing. The existence of all these companies depends on the protection of their inventions. Otherwise, anyone could make a knockoff iPhone or replicate a Boeing 737 plane and sell it on the market. In that case, these companies would not be able to sustain themselves and cover the costs of their research and development units.
The preservation of intellectual property rights is at the core of American innovation.

One criticism of the above paragraph could be that it presents a somewhat one-sided view of the role of intellectual property rights in promoting innovation and entrepreneurship in the United States. While it is true that such rights have played an important role in protecting and incentivizing inventors and businesses, it is also important to acknowledge that there have been many cases where these rights have been abused or misused. For example, there have been numerous instances where large corporations have used their financial and legal resources to unfairly dominate smaller competitors or to stifle innovation by enforcing overly broad patents or copyrights. Moreover, some critics argue that the current system of intellectual property rights in the US actually hinders rather than encourages innovation by creating unnecessary barriers to entry and limiting the free flow of information and ideas.[224] In light of these concerns, it is important to recognize that while intellectual property rights can be a valuable tool for promoting innovation and entrepreneurship, they are not without their drawbacks and limitations.[225]

3.1.13.1 Criticism to Property Rights

While the protection of property rights is generally seen as a cornerstone of American entrepreneurship, it has also been a source of criticism. One major criticism is the way that property rights have been used to stifle innovation and limit competition. This has been seen particularly in the realm of intellectual property, where large corporations have used patents and copyrights to prevent smaller competitors from entering the market.

For example, in the early days of the automobile industry, a number of manufacturers held patents on key components,[226] such as the steering wheel, that prevented other companies from producing similar cars. This stifled innovation and slowed the development of the industry as a whole. Similarly, in the tech industry, there have been numerous lawsuits over patent infringement that have limited competition and innovation.

Another criticism of property rights in the context of entrepreneurship is the way they can be used to exploit

---

[224] Jason Wiens and Chris Jackson, "How Intellectual Property Can Help or Hinder Innovation," Harvard Business Review, April 6, 2015.

[225] Boldrin, Michele, and David K. Levine. "The case against patents." Journal of Economic Perspectives 27.1 (2013): 3-22.

[226] Smith, Angella LaNette. "Patent Appeal: The Protection of Intellectual Property Rights in the American Automotive Sector, 1903-1911." Michigan Historical Review 49.1 (2023): 99-127.

natural resources and damage the environment.[227] When property rights are used to justify the unrestricted exploitation of natural resources, it can have serious consequences for the environment and future generations.

For example, in the 19th century, wealthy landowners in the American West were able to acquire vast tracts of land, often at the expense of Native American communities.[228] This led to the overgrazing of livestock, the depletion of water resources, and the destruction of the natural environment. Similarly, today, some large corporations are accused of exploiting natural resources in ways that are harmful to the environment and future generations.

Overall, while property rights are an important aspect of American entrepreneurship, there are valid criticisms that they can be used to limit competition and innovation, as well as to exploit natural resources and damage the environment. It is important for entrepreneurs and policymakers to consider these criticisms and work towards a more balanced approach to property rights that benefits both individuals and society as a whole.

3.1.12.2 Property Rights in Europe

Throughout European history, property rights, including intellectual and physical property, have played a crucial role in shaping society and influencing entrepreneurship and innovation. The development of property rights in Europe can be understood within its historical context, spanning from the 17th century to the present day.

---

[227] McKern, Bruce, ed. *Transnational corporations and the exploitation of natural resources*. Vol. 10. Taylor & Francis, 1993.

[228] Johansen, Bruce E. *Resource exploitation in Native North America: a plague upon the Peoples*. Bloomsbury Publishing USA, 2016.

During the 17th and 18th centuries, Europe experienced significant social and economic transformations, including the rise of mercantilism and the Industrial Revolution.[229] These changes brought about a shift in the understanding and recognition of property rights. The emergence of capitalist systems and the growth of trade and commerce led to an increased emphasis on private property rights as a means to facilitate economic growth. Influenced by philosophers like John Locke, Europe began to recognize the importance of individual property rights as a foundation for personal liberty and economic prosperity.

In the 19th century, Europe witnessed further developments in property rights as industrialization progressed. The expansion of factories, mines, and railroads required clear property rights to enable investment, secure loans, and establish contracts. Legal frameworks were established to protect physical property, allowing entrepreneurs to accumulate and utilize assets for entrepreneurial activities. Intellectual property rights also gained importance during this period, with the advent of patents and copyright laws to encourage innovation and protect the rights of inventors and creators.

However, it is important to acknowledge that property rights in Europe were not uniform across the continent. Different countries and regions adopted varying legal frameworks and traditions, leading to diverse approaches to property rights. For example, common law systems,[230] influenced by English legal traditions, emphasized individual property rights and

---

[229] Berlanstein, Lenard R., ed. *The industrial revolution and work in nineteenth century Europe*. Routledge, 2003.

[230] Amos, Maurice Sheldon. "The common law and the civil law in the British Commonwealth of nations." *Harv. L. Rev.* 50 (1936): 1249.

provided a strong foundation for entrepreneurship and innovation. Civil law systems, prevalent in continental Europe, focused on codified laws and principles that governed property rights, offering stability and predictability for economic activities.

In the aftermath of World War II, Europe witnessed the formation of supranational organizations such as the European Union (EU), which sought to harmonize laws and regulations across member states. The EU's establishment of intellectual property rights, such as the European Patent Office and the EU Copyright Directive, aimed to create a unified framework for protecting intellectual property and fostering innovation within Europe.

Additionally, Europe's history and cultural diversity have influenced property rights in various ways. In some regions, collective or communal property arrangements[231] have been prominent, particularly in rural or agrarian communities. These arrangements reflect the historical practices of shared land and resource management, aligning with cultural values and community-oriented approaches to property rights.

In recent years, Europe has faced new challenges and opportunities with the digital age and the increasing importance of intellectual property in the knowledge economy. The rise of digital platforms, e-commerce, and intangible assets has prompted Europe to adapt its legal and regulatory frameworks to address emerging issues and protect intellectual property in the digital realm.[232]

---

[231] Eggertsson, Thrainn. "The economic rationale of communal resources." *Law and the governance of renewable resources: Studies from northern Europe and Africa* (1998).

[232] Senftleben, Martin. "Adapting EU Trademark Law to New Technologies-Back to Basics?." *Constructing European Intellectual Property: Achievements and New Perspectives, C. Geiger, ed., Edward Elgar Publishing* (2013).

In conclusion, property rights have played a significant role in shaping European societies and influencing entrepreneurship and innovation throughout history. The recognition and protection of both intellectual and physical property have provided a foundation for economic growth, individual liberty, and creative endeavors. Europe's diverse legal systems, cultural norms, and historical experiences have contributed to variations in property rights across the continent. Understanding the historical context of property rights in Europe helps shed light on their importance and impact on entrepreneurship and innovation within the region

The greatness of America lies not in being more enlightened than any other nation, but rather in her ability to repair her faults.
Alexis de Tocqueville

4. CONCLUSION: EVALUATION OF UNIFYING AMERICAN VALUES AND ELEMENTS THAT SHAPE THE AMERICAN ENTREPRENEURIAL SPIRIT

Freedom of thought, freedom of speech, freedom to undertake ventures, equality before the law, equal opportunities, absence of oppression by privileged individuals, ownership of property and homeland, a philosophy that values hard work and saving, an active lifestyle that emphasizes achieving results, a culture that values the protection of ideas, a population that constantly seeks innovation and pushes boundaries, and individuals who believe they can achieve their dreams if they pursue them are the hallmarks of a country with a large enough scale to allow for economies of scale, where entrepreneurs can create global industries.

The drive for pioneering and pushing beyond borders in America has led to the continuous expansion of geographic boundaries, which in turn has manifested itself in technology, science, art, lifestyle, and business models.

Creativity and innovation are two concepts that are inseparable from American culture, forming the foundation of pushing beyond borders. Americans have often solved problems by adopting ideas they've seen elsewhere or by coming up with completely new ideas. They've been successful in innovating by disseminating their inventions and discoveries. For example, they not only invented the light bulb, but they also revolutionized social life by bringing it into every home.

Risk-taking is at the core of pushing beyond borders, pioneering, creativity, and innovation. Without the ability to take risks, it is impossible to try something new, go beyond the familiar and known, or relinquish what one has in order to create something new. The American characteristic of being able to take risks has made it possible to accomplish feats such as building the first airplane or going to the moon, leaving Harvard and other prestigious institutions to become an entrepreneur.

Competition and renewal act as a type of immune system in American society. Competition keeps American society constantly on its toes, driving individuals and institutions to continuously seek improvement and renewal in order to be better than others. Microsoft's continuous improvement can be attributed to Apple's presence, while Google's constant innovation is due to Yahoo's existence. Competition in education and the workplace leads to innovation in all areas in America.

Meritocracy-based social structure is one of the fundamental features of America. In America, talent, project experience, and the ability to deliver results are more important than family ties, connections to top-level executives, bureaucrats, and politicians, and even diplomas. Society continually elevates university graduates, the best among them, those without degrees but who can complete projects and deliver results. Bill Gates, Steve Jobs, and Howard Schultz are evaluated based on their ability to do business without considering their educational background or where they came from, and they are given opportunities to work where their skills are needed.

The greatest wealth of America lies in the concept of the American Dream. Regardless of their origin, education, or starting conditions, every American citizen believes they can be highly successful in their chosen field based on their abilities, creativity, hard work, and the scope of their project. In a country where, just a few decades ago, black people were forced to enter buses from the back door, Barack Obama, a black man, not only graduated from Harvard University but also became the President of the United States. The concepts of American individualism and self-reliance have also shaped American society and entrepreneurship. As Ralph Waldo Emerson stated, "Only those who can create unity from diversity can have authority." Therefore, American individualism is based on both pursuing one's own choices and organizing oneself as a guarantee of those choices. While pursuing their personal dreams and interests, American entrepreneurs also serve society by transforming it through their dreams and actions.

Another important aspect that complements the concepts of meritocracy, the American Dream, and American individualism is the idea of the self-made person. In a country where equal opportunities exist, it doesn't matter how difficult a person's start in life was. American culture and the system allow a creative individual with talents, dreams, and passions to achieve great success without any help from anyone, in line with their abilities and projects. Despite being removed from formal education and being born into a low-income family, Thomas Edison was able to achieve significant economic success as well as make great inventions.

American entrepreneurs come from diverse ethnic backgrounds, some being immigrants themselves or the children of immigrants. Despite this, they consider America their homeland and work to serve American society. Max Weber's Protestant work ethic has instilled a sense of hard work in American society. Regardless of whether they go to church or not, or whether they are Christians or not, American entrepreneurs are hardworking and action-oriented individuals. Projects such as Facebook, the lightbulb, automobiles, airplanes, computers, thousands of kilometers of railways, millions of drawings in animations, and amusement parks that cover millions of square meters could not have been completed without hard work.

One of the biggest characteristics that sets America apart from the rest of the world is that decision-makers and industry-creating entrepreneurs make decisions in accordance with the philosophy of pragmatism. They choose actions based on their results, not universal definitions. For example, dropping out of school is universally seen as a bad decision, but if dropping out of school leads to achieving global success as an entrepreneur, then it becomes a good decision. Particularly, American entrepreneurs who create industries make decisions through pragmatic evaluations.

America's greatest wealth is the concept of the American Dream. Regardless of their origins, education, or starting conditions, every American citizen believes that they can be extremely successful in their chosen field based on their talent, creativity, hard work, and the scale of their projects. In a country where black people were forced to enter the back of buses in the 1950s, Barack Obama, a black man, not only graduated from Harvard University, but also became the President of the United States. The founders of the WhatsApp application, Brian Acton and Jan Koum, became billionaires after founding their company in 2009.

American individualism is also one of the factors that shape American society and entrepreneurs. According to Ralph Waldo Emerson's proposition, "Only those who can create unity by separating can have authority." American individualism is based on pursuing one's own choices and organizing to secure them. While chasing their personal dreams and interests, American entrepreneurs also serve society by pursuing their dreams and actions, transforming society.

Meritocracy, the American Dream, and American individualism are complemented by the concept of the self-made individual. In a country where equal opportunities are developed, it does not matter how unsuitable a person's circumstances are for their talents, dreams, and passions. American culture and system allow a creative individual who pursues their dreams to achieve great success without help. Despite being expelled from formal education and coming from a low-income family, Thomas Edison achieved both economic success and made significant contributions to science and innovation.

All American entrepreneurs come from families with different ethnic backgrounds. Some of them are immigrants themselves. Nevertheless, they considered America their home and worked to serve American society.

Max Weber's Protestant work ethic instilled a sense of diligence in American society. American entrepreneurs are diligent and active individuals, whether they go to church or not. Projects such as Facebook, the light bulb, cars, planes, computers, thousands of kilometers of railways, millions of drawings comprising animations, and millions of square meters of amusement parks cannot be achieved without hard work.

One of the biggest differences between America and Europe is that while only one language is spoken in America, twenty-five languages are used for communication in Europe. Despite the existence of the European Union, the presence of borders does not allow for the free movement of people and goods as it does in America. Europe's deep class structure has not been eradicated despite all efforts to democratize society. An ideal like the American Dream is not shared in Europe. In addition, European individualism is sharply defined and can work against the interests of society or the country, unlike in America. In the European Union, composed of different nations, every nation considers leaving the Union at the slightest problem, whereas in America, communities with different ethnic backgrounds have been integrated and closely connected. When evaluated from these perspectives, it becomes clear why all the world's major industries began in America. Because only America possesses this set of conditions mentioned in this work.

Canada, which has a similar characteristic as Europe, cannot be compared to America in terms of its conditions, given its population of 30 million and two spoken languages. Similarly, Australia, with a population of 22 million, is not suitable for comparison primarily due to its small scale. For countries with geographical sizes proportional to that of America, such as Russia, India, and China, many of the conditions that make up the American Context are absent. To analyze these countries, it is necessary to examine their own unique contexts.

Therefore, the effort to go beyond borders, melting pot, individualism, American Dream, creativity and innovation, self-made individual, competition and renewal, pragmatism, strong religious beliefs that support work and accumulation, private property rights, and intellectual property rights all together create an environment for industrial entrepreneurs to emerge in a country.

Sources

About Renault, https://www.renault.com.eg/AboutRenault/Renault-history.html, retrieved on September 21, 2023.

Acemoglu, Daron, and James A. Robinson. Why Nations Fail: The Origins of Power, Prosperity, and Poverty. New York: Crown, 2012.

Acquisition and Retention of U.S. Citizenship and Nationality. U.S. Department of State. http://www.state.gov/documents/organization/86755.pdf. (10.07.2011).

Alexis de Tocqueville, Democracy in America, Penguin Classics, 2003.

Allen, Robert. "Capital accumulation, technological change, and the distribution of income during the British Industrial Revolution." (2005).

Amos, Maurice Sheldon. "The common law and the civil law in the British Commonwealth of nations." Harv. L. Rev. 50 (1936): 1249.

Bacon, Michael. Pragmatism: an introduction. Polity, 2012.

Balady, Gary J. "Survival of the fittest — more evidence." New England Journal of Medicine 346.11 (2002): 852-854.

Balinska, Maria. The bagel: The surprising history of a modest bread. Yale University Press, 2008.

Banner, Stuart. American property: A history of how, why, and what we own. Harvard University Press, 2011.

Barnham, Kay. Thomas Edison. Capstone Classroom, 2014.

Bashir, Hilal, and Shabir Ahmad Bhat. "Effects of social media on mental health: A review." International Journal of Indian Psychology 4.3 (2017): 125-131.

Bell, James, and Jelmer Stellingwerf. "Sustainable entrepreneurship: The motivations and challenges

of sustainable entrepreneurs in the renewable
energy industry." (2012).

Berawi, Mohammed Ali. "Quality revolution: leading
the innovation and competitive advantages."
International Journal of Quality & Reliability
Management 21.4 (2004): 425-438.

Berlanstein, Lenard R., ed. The industrial revolution and
work in nineteenth century Europe. Routledge,
2003.

Bernard Marrey, The Extraordinary Life and Work of
Monsieur Gustave Eiffel, the Engineer Who Built
the Statue of Liberty, the Porto Bridge, the Nice
Observatory, the ... the Panama Locks, the Eiffel
Tower, etc., Graphite Publications, January 1,
1984.

Bernstein, Peter L., and Peter L. Bernstein. Against the
gods: The remarkable story of risk. New York:
Wiley, 1996.

Bidwell, Percy Wells, and John Ironside Falconer.
History of agriculture in the northern United
States, 1620-1860. No. 358. Carnegie Institution of
Washington, 1925.

Biggest Countries,
http://geography.about.com/od/countryinforma
tion/a/bigcountries.htm, (10.07.2011).

Binford, Jason B. "The Role of Federal and State
Regulators in Crypto Bankruptcies." American
Bankruptcy Institute Journal 42.5 (2023): 28-48.

Birkinshaw, Julian. "Entrepreneurship in the global
firm: Enterprise and renewal." Entrepreneurship
in the Global Firm (2000): 1-168.

Boldrin, Michele, and David K. Levine. "The case
against patents." Journal of Economic Perspectives
27.1 (2013): 3-22.

Bonney, Richard. Economic systems and state finance:
The origins of the modern state in Europe 13th to
18th centuries. Oxford University Press, 1995.

Boyer, Allen D. Sir Edward Coke and the Elizabethan Age. Stanford University Press, 2003.

Brad, Stone, The Everything Store: Jeff Bezos and the Age of Amazon, Little, Brown and Company, 2013.

Brands, Henry William. The first American: The life and times of Benjamin Franklin. Anchor, 2010.

Brenner, Robert. "Feudalism." Marxian Economics. London: Palgrave Macmillan UK, 1990. 170-185.

Brown, Jennifer K. "The Nineteenth Amendment and women's equality." The Yale Law Journal 102.8 (1993): 2175-2204.

Buccola, Nicholas. ""The Essential Dignity of Man as Man": Frederick Douglass on Human Dignity." American Political Thought 4.2 (2015): 228-258.

Burlingame, Roger., Benjamin Franklin, Envoy Extraordinary, Coward-McCann, New York, 1967, p. 36.

Caliendo, Stephen. Inequality in America: Race, poverty, and fulfilling democracy's promise. Routledge, 2021.

Caliendo, Stephen. Inequality in America: Race, poverty, and fulfilling democracy's promise. Routledge, 2021.

Carnegie, Andrew HG. The gospel of wealth, and other timely essays. Harvard University Press, 1962.

Case, Karl E., Ray C. Fair, and Sharon M. Oster. Principles of Economics. 10th ed., NJ: Prentice Hall, 2012. p. 49.

Cashman, Sean Dennis. America in the gilded age. NYU Press, 1993.

Chamberlain, ibid, p. XIV.

Chamberlain, John. The Enterprising Americans: A Chronicle of Business Enterprise. New York: Harper & Brothers, 1963. Print.

Charles Robert Darwin, The Origin of Species. Vol. XI. The Harvard Classics. New York: P.F. Collier & Son, 1909-14; Bartleby.com, 2001.

Charles Sanders Peirce: Pragmatism, https://iep.utm.edu/peircepr, Retrieved on September, 20, 2023.

Chen, Yang, Liang Cheng, and Chien-Chiang Lee. "How does the use of industrial robots affect the ecological footprint? International evidence." Ecological Economics 198 (2022): 107483.

Chinese Exclusion Act (1882), An act to execute certain treaty stipulations relating to the Chinese, May 6, 1882; Enrolled Acts and Resolutions of Congress, 1789-1996; General Records of the United States Government; Record Group 11; National Archives https://www.archives.gov/milestone-documents/chinese-exclusion-act

Chirinko, Robert S., and Daniel J. Wilson. "Tax competition among US states: Racing to the bottom or riding on a seesaw?." Journal of Public Economics 155 (2017): 147-163.

Christensen, Clay, Michael E. Raynor, and Rory McDonald. Disruptive innovation. Brighton, MA, USA: Harvard Business Review, 2013.

Claude Fischer, American individualism – really? The evidence that we are not who we think we are, http://blogs.berkeley.edu/2010/04/20/american-individualism-%E2%80%93-really, (30.08.2011).

Costa, Carlos M., et al. "Recycling and environmental issues of lithium-ion batteries: Advances, challenges and opportunities." Energy Storage Materials 37 (2021): 433-465.

Croucher, Stephen M., and Eric Kramer. "Cultural fusion theory: An alternative to acculturation." Journal of International and Intercultural Communication 10.2 (2017): 97-114.

Crouzet, François. A History of the European Economy, 1000-2000: 1000-2000. University of Virginia Press, 2001.

Crowell, Ethan. Weber's "Protestant ethic" and his critics. The University of Texas at Arlington, 2006.

Curley, Martin, et al. "Digital disruption." Open Innovation 2.0: The New Mode of Digital Innovation for Prosperity and Sustainability (2018): 15-25.

Daniels, Norman. "Merit and meritocracy." Philosophy & Public Affairs (1978): 206-223.

David Galenson, Old Masters and Young Geniuses, Princeton, 2005.

Davies, Scott, and Floyd M. Hammack. "The channeling of student competition in higher education: Comparing Canada and the US." The Journal of Higher Education 76.1 (2005): 89-106.

de Crevoecoeur, J. Hector St John. Letters from an American Farmer. Prabhat Prakashan, 2021.

De Tocqueville, Alexis. Democracy in America-Vol. I. and II. Read Books Ltd, 2015.

Delgado, Leticia. "Immigration in Europe: realities and policies." (2002).

Dewald, Jonathan. The European Nobility, 1400-1800. Vol. 9. Cambridge University Press, 1996, pg. 12-14.

Dewald, Jonathan. The European Nobility, 1400-1800. Vol. 9. Cambridge University Press, 1996.

Diamond, Jared M. Guns, Germs, and Steel: The Fates of Human Societies. New York: W. W. Norton & Company, 1997.

Diren Çakmak, Osmanlı Telif Hukuku ile İlgili Mevzuat, Türkiyat Araştırmaları Dergisi, sayı: 21. http://www.turkiyat.selcuk.edu.tr/pdfdergi/s21/cakmak.pdf, (20.08.2011). Diren Çakmak, Osmanlı Telif Hukuku ile İlgili Mevzuat, Türkiyat Araştırmaları Dergisi, sayı: 21.

http://www.turkiyat.selcuk.edu.tr/pdfdergi/s21
/cakmak.pdf, (20.08.2011).

Donald Barlett, James B. Steele, The Betrayal of the
American Dream, Public Affairs, 2012.

Douglass, Frederick. Self-made men. CreateSpace
Independent Publishing Platform, 2015.

Drucker, Peter F. Innovation and Entrepreneurship:
Practice and Principles. New York:
HarperBusiness, 1999. Print. p. 20.

Durant, Will, and Ariel Durant. The Age of reason
begins: a history of European civilization in the
period of Shakespeare, Bacon, Montaigne,
Rembrandt, Galileo, and Descartes: 1558-1648.
Simon and Schuster, 1961.

Edward Grabb, Douglas Baer, and James Curtis, The
Origins of American Individualism: Reconsidering
the Historical Evidence, Canadian Journal of
Sociology, 24, 4, 1999, s.511-533.

Eggers, J. P., and Lin Song. "Dealing with failure: Serial
entrepreneurs and the costs of changing industries
between ventures." Academy of Management
Journal 58.6 (2015): 1785-1803.

Eggertsson, Thrainn. "The economic rationale of
communal resources." Law and the governance of
renewable resources: Studies from northern
Europe and Africa (1998).

Eidlin, Barry. "Class vs. special interest: labor, power,
and politics in the United States and Canada in the
twentieth century." Politics & Society 43.2 (2015):
181-211.

Emerson, Ralph Waldo, and Richard Wulf. Self-reliance.
Caxton Society, 1909.

Esch, Elizabeth. The color line and the assembly line:
Managing race in the Ford empire. Vol. 50. Univ
of California Press, 2018.

Evens, Tom, et al. Winner Takes All. Springer
International Publishing, 2018.

Farinha, Luís, João JM Ferreira, and Sara Nunes. "Linking innovation and entrepreneurship to economic growth." Competitiveness Review: An International Business Journal 28.4 (2018): 451-475.

Fortnow, Matt, and QuHarrison Terry. The NFT Handbook: How to create, sell and buy non-fungible tokens. John Wiley & Sons, 2021.

Franklin, Benjamin. "Advice to a Young Tradesman, (21 July 1748)". Founders Online. National Archives and Records Administration/University of Virginia Press. Archived from the original on August 23, 2019. Retrieved November 1, 2019.

Franklin, Benjamin. Poor Richard's almanack. Barnes & Noble Publishing, 2004.

Franklin, Benjamin. The Autobiography of Benjamin Franklin. Vol. 41. PF Collier, 1909.

Franklin, John Hope. "History of racial segregation in the United States." The ANNALS of the American Academy of Political and Social Science 304.1 (1956): 1-9.

Frederick Jackson Turner, The Significance of the Frontier in American History, Penguin Great Ideas, 2008.

Frequently Asked Questions: Patents, World Intellectual Property Organization, https://www.wipo.int/patents/en/faq_patents.html, retrieved on September 20, 2023.

Freyer, F. F., & Saltzman, J. (2020, May 19). 'This is not how you do science': Cambridge biotech Moderna's potential COVID-19 vaccine stirs hope — and criticism. The Boston Globe. Retrieved from https://www.bostonglobe.com/2020/05/19/business/hope-covid-19-vaccine-attracts-investors-cambridge-biotech/

Galloway, Scott. The four: the hidden DNA of Amazon, Apple, Facebook, and Google. Penguin, 2018.

Garrett, Leslie. DK Readers L4: First Flight: The Story of the Wright Brothers. Penguin, 2012.

Gary Hamel, Bill Breen, The Future of Management, Harvard Business Review Press, 2007, p.174.

Gaur, Bhawna. "The Dark Side of Leadership." Global Leadership Perspectives on Industry, Society, and Government in an Era of Uncertainty. IGI Global, 2023. 176-201.

Geibel, Richard C., and Meghana Manickam. "Comparison of selected startup ecosystems in Germany and in the USA Explorative analysis of the startup environments." GSTF Journal on Business Review (GBR) 4.3 (2016).

George Lucas, dir. Star Wars: A New Hope. 1977; Beverly Hills, CA: 20th Century Fox, 2011.

Gerald Gunderson, The Wealth Creators An Entrepreneurial History of the United States,Truman Talley Books, 1989, s.1.

Gioia, Ted. The history of jazz. Oxford University Press, 2011.

Giorgi, Liana, and Catherine Marsh. "The Protestant work ethic as a cultural phenomenon." European Journal of Social Psychology 20.6 (1990): 499-517.

GORDON, MILTON. "E Pluribus Unum? The myth of the melting pot." American Studies | Volume (2014): 257.

Gunderson, ibid, p.7.

Gusterson, Gerald. The Wealth Creators: The Rise of Venture Capital and the Fall of the Middle Class. New York: Picador, 2017. Print.

Hall, Fred. The rise of startup hubs in Europe: a qualitative study on the factors contributing to Berlin's rise as a european startup hub. Diss. 2016.

Harari, Yuval Noah. Sapiens: A Brief History of Humankind. New York: Harper Perennial, 2015.

Hart, David M., and Zoltan J. Acs. "High-tech immigrant entrepreneurship in the United States."

Economic Development Quarterly 25.2 (2011): 116-129.n

Hatton, Timothy J., and Jeffrey G. Williamson. "What drove the mass migrations from Europe in the late nineteenth century?." (1992).

Heckscher, Eli F. Mercantilism. Routledge, 2013.

Helstosky, Carol. Pizza: a global history. Reaktion books, 2008.

Hippel, Eric Von, Democratizing Innovation, MIT Press, 2006.

Holub, Joan, and H. Q. Who. What was the Gold Rush?. Penguin, 2013.

Holweg, Matthias. "The evolution of competition in the automotive industry." Build to order: The road to the 5-day car. London: Springer London, 2008. 13-34.

Imai, Masaaki. Kaizen. Vol. 201. New York: Random House Business Division, 1986.

Isaacson, Walter. Steve Jobs. Simon & Schuster, 2011.

Jacobs, Margaret D. White mother to a dark race: Settler colonialism, maternalism, and the removal of Indigenous children in the American West and Australia, 1880-1940. U of Nebraska Press, 2009.

James Truslow Adams, The Epic of America, Blue Ribbon Books, New York, 1931.

Jason Wiens and Chris Jackson, "How Intellectual Property Can Help or Hinder Innovation," Harvard Business Review, April 6, 2015.

Jim Cullen, The American dream: a short history of an idea that shaped a nation, Oxford University Press US, 2004, sf. 3.

Johansen, Bruce E. Resource exploitation in Native North America: a plague upon the Peoples. Bloomsbury Publishing USA, 2016.

John Dewey, Stanford Encyclopedia of Philosophy, https://plato.stanford.edu/entries/dewey/, retrieved on September 21, 2023.

John Kadvany,Baruch Fishoff, Risk: A Brief Introduction, OUP Oxford, 2011.

Johne Locke, Two Treaties of Goverment, Cambridge University Press, 1988, s.184.

Johnson, Michelle T., The Diversity Code: Unlock the Secrets to Making Differences Work in the Real World, Amacom, 2010.

Joseph J. C. Hobbs, Fundamentals of World Regional Geography (Cengage, 2017), 114.

Keeley, Larry, et al. Ten types of innovation: The discipline of building breakthroughs. John Wiley & Sons, 2013.

Kennedy, Debbie, Putting Our Differences to Work: The Fastest Way to Innovation, Leadership, and High Performance, Berret Koehler Business, 2008.

Kennedy, Paul M. The Rise and Fall of the Great Powers: Economic Change and Military Conflict from 1500 to 2000. New York: Random House, 1987.

Kingston, Paul F. "Long-term environmental impact of oil spills." Spill Science & Technology Bulletin 7.1-2 (2002): 53-61.

Klein, Maury. The change makers: from Carnegie to Gates, how the great entrepreneurs transformed ideas into industries. Macmillan, 2003.

Kleon, Austin. Steal Like an Artist 10th Anniversary Gift Edition with a New Afterword by the Author: 10 Things Nobody Told You About Being Creative. Workman Publishing, 2022.

Koch, Malina. "Tech Start-up Internationalisation: Development of an internationalisation model for born global web-based tech start-ups from European start-up hubs." (2017).

Kubin, Emily, and Christian von Sikorski. "The role of (social) media in political polarization: a systematic review." Annals of the International Communication Association 45.3 (2021): 188-206.

Landes, David S. The Wealth and Poverty of Nations: Why Some Are So Rich and Some So Poor. 1st ed. New York: W. W. Norton & Company, 1998.

Laurie Carlson, Thomas Edison: His Life and Ideas, Chicago Review Press, 2006, pg. 116.

Lécuyer, Christophe. Making Silicon Valley: Innovation and the growth of high tech, 1930-1970. MIT Press, 2006.

Lehrer, Jonah. Imagine: How creativity works. Houghton Mifflin Harcourt, 2012.

Levine, George. Darwin loves you: natural selection and the re-enchantment of the world. Princeton University Press, 2008.

Lewis, Michael M. The new new thing: A Silicon Valley story. WW Norton & Company, 2000.

Locke, John. "Natural rights." Moral Reasoning: A Philosophic Approach to Applied Ethics, Dryden Press, London (1990): 133-5.

Loewen, James W. Lies my teacher told me: Everything your American history textbook got wrong. The New Press, 2008.

Magnusson, Lars. Routledge Explorations in Economic History: Political Economy of Mercantilism. Taylor & Francis, 2015.

Mankiw, N. Gregory. Principles of Economics. 10th ed. Boston: Cengage, 2021. Print. p. 20.

Mann, Michael. The sources of social power: volume 2, the rise of classes and nation-states, 1760-1914. Vol. 2. Cambridge University Press, 2012.

Manuel, Frank E. The age of reason. Cornell University Press, 2019.

Marie, Luzia. "The Dynamics of European Startup Hubs." (2016).

Mark Robert Rank, Thomas A. Hirschl, Kirk A. Foster, Chasing the American Dream, Oxford University Press, 2014.

Markus Hearn, Ron Howard, The Cinema of George Lucas, Harry N. Abrams, 2005.

Maxwell, Claire, and Peter Aggleton, eds. Elite education: International perspectives. Routledge, 2015.

McClure, Paul K. ""You're fired," says the robot: The rise of automation in the workplace, technophobes, and fears of unemployment." Social Science Computer Review 36.2 (2018): 139-156.

McGee, John S. "Predatory price cutting: the Standard Oil (NJ) case." The Journal of Law and Economics 1 (1958): 137-169.

McGregor, Moira, Barry Brown, and Mareike Glöss. "Disrupting the cab: Uber, ridesharing and the taxi industry." Journal of Peer Production 6 (2015).

McKern, Bruce, ed. Transnational corporations and the exploitation of natural resources. Vol. 10. Taylor & Francis, 1993.

McKibben, Gordon. Cutting Edge: Gilette's Journey to Global Leadership, Harvard Business Review Books, 1997.

McManus, James. "An essay review of: THE TESTING TRAP by Andrew J. Strenio, Jr." The Review of Higher Education 5.1 (1981): 49.

Michel, Gwendolyn M., et al. "Stories we wear: Promoting sustainability practices with the case of Patagonia." Family and Consumer Sciences Research Journal 48.2 (2019): 165-180.

Mitchell, Julia Post. St. Jean de Crèvecoeur. Columbia University Press, 1916.

Mudrack, Peter E. "Protestant work-ethic dimensions and work orientations." Personality and individual differences 23.2 (1997): 217-225.

Murray, David Kord. Borrowing brilliance: the six steps to business innovation by building on the ideas of others. penguin, 2009.

Natural Resources in the US,
http://geography.about.com/library/cia/blcusa.
htm, (10.07.2011).

Neckerman, Kathryn, ed. Social inequality. Russell Sage
Foundation, 2004.

Nelson, Michael. "A short, ironic history of American
national bureaucracy." The Journal of Politics 44.3
(1982): 747-778.

Nelson, Robert H. "Is Max Weber Newly Relevant?: The
Protestant-Catholic Divide in Europe Today."
Finnish Journal of Theology 5 (2012).

Németh, Ádám, et al. "Competing diversity índices and
attitudes toward cultural pluralism in Europe."
Equality, Diversity and Inclusion: An
International Journal 41.7 (2022): 1029-1046.

Nica, Elvira. "Will robots take the jobs of human
workers? Disruptive technologies that may bring
about jobless growth and enduring mass
unemployment." Psychosociological Issues in
Human Resource Management 6.2 (2018): 56-61.

Nicole Mitchel, Pendleton Civil Service Act, Amazon
Digital Services, 2013.

Noll, A. Michael. The evolution of media. Rowman &
Littlefield, 2007.

Nye, David E. America's assembly line. MIT Press, 2013.

Orville Wright, Rupert Holland, The Story of the Wright
Brothers and the Flying Machine, Cornell
Publications, 2011.

Outram, Dorinda. The enlightenment. Cambridge
University Press, 2019.

Outram, Dorinda. The enlightenment. Cambridge
University Press, 2019.

Owen, David. Copies in Seconds: How a Lone Inventor
and an Unknown Company Created the Biggest
Communication Breakthrough Since Gutenberg--
Chester Carlson and the Birth of the Xerox
Machine. Simon and Schuster, 2008.

Page, William H., and John E. Lopatka. The Microsoft case: antitrust, high technology, and consumer welfare. University of Chicago Press, 2009.

Paine, Robert T., et al. "Trouble on oiled waters: lessons from the Exxon Valdez oil spill." Annual Review of Ecology and Systematics 27.1 (1996): 197-235.

Parker, Michael. John Winthrop: founding the city upon a hill. Routledge, 2013.

Parmy Olson, "Facebook Closes $19 Billion WhatsApp Deal," Forbes, October 6, 2014, https://www.forbes.com/sites/parmyolson/2014/10/06/facebook-closes-19-billion-whatsapp-deal/?sh=7b69869a5c66.

Paul Burns, Entrepreneurship and Small Business, Palgrave, London, 2001, s. 4.

Persson, Karl Gunnar, and Paul Sharp. An economic history of Europe. Cambridge University Press, 2015.

Peter Drucker, ibid. p. 23.

Peter Sims, Little Bets, How Breakthrough Ideas Emerge from Small Discoveries, Simon Schuster, 2013.

Peukert, Helge. "Mercantilism." Handbook of the History of Economic Thought: Insights on the Founders of Modern Economics. New York, NY: Springer New York, 2011. 93-121.

Philip P. Wiener, Evolution and the Founders of Pragmatism, Peter Smith Pub., 1969.

Pickett, Kate, and Richard Wilkinson. The Spirit Level: Why More Equal Societies Almost Always Do Better. London: Allen Lane, 2009.

Po Bronson, "HotMale: Sabeer Bhatia started his company on USD 300.000 and sold it two years later for USD 400 million. So is he lucky or great?, Wired, Issue, 6.12 December 1998.

Porter, Gayle. "Work, work ethic, work excess." Journal of organizational change management 17.5 (2004): 424-439.

PRAGMATISM --- WHAT IT IS --- BY PROF WILLIAM JAMES; Harvard Philosopher Explains that His Stand Is Entirely for "a Philosophy That Works" and a Man Who Shapes His Own Fate. A Skepticism Which Sees the Impossibility to the Human Mind of Attaining Real Truth, So Studies the Laws of Phenomena. New York Times Interview, published on November 3, 1907, https://www.nytimes.com/1907/11/03/archives/pragmatism-what-it-is-by-prof-william-james-harvard-philosopher.html?searchResultPosition=19

Pragmatism, Stanford Encyclopedia of Philosophy, https://plato.stanford.edu/index.html, retrieved on September 21, 2023.

Prokop, Daniel. "University entrepreneurial ecosystems and spinoff companies: Configurations, developments and outcomes." Technovation 107 (2021): 102286.

Purvis, Thomas L. Colonial America to 1763. Infobase Publishing, 2014.

Ralph Waldo Emerson, Essays, http://www.gutenberg.org/etext/2944, (24.12.2011).

Ray Kroc ve Robert Anderson, Grinding It Out: The Making Of McDonald's,Saint Martin's Paperbacks, Saint Martin, 1992.

Richard ve Ramesh Ponnuru. "An Exceptional Debate: The Obama Administration's Assault on American identity." National Review, 8 Mart 2010, Cilt.62, Sayı.2, s.18-20.

Rifkin, Jeremy. The European dream: How Europe's vision of the future is quietly eclipsing the American dream. John Wiley & Sons, 2013.

Robert Park, E. Burgess ve R. McKenzie, The City, University of Chicago Press, 1925, p.41.

Schumpeter, Joseph A. "Entrepreneurship as innovation." University of Illinois at Urbana-Champaign's Academy for Entrepreneurial Leadership Historical Research Reference in Entrepreneurship (2000).

Schweikart, Larry, and Lynne Doti. American Entrepreneur: A History of Business in the United States. Amacom, 2009, pg. 81-82.

Senftleben, Martin. "Adapting EU Trademark Law to New Technologies-Back to Basics?." Constructing European Intellectual Property: Achievements and New Perspectives, C. Geiger, ed., Edward Elgar Publishing (2013).

Sherman, Josepha. Jeff Bezos: King of Amazon. Twenty-First Century Books, 2001.

Silverman, Dan P. Reconstructing Europe after the Great War. Harvard University Press, 1982.

Simpson, Barbara. "Pragmatism: A philosophy of practice." The SAGE handbook of qualitative business and management research methods (2018): 54-68.

Size of Europe, http://www.world-atlas.us/europe.htm, (10.07.2011).

Smith, Adam. The wealth of nations [1776]. Vol. 11937. na, 1937.

Smith, Angella LaNette. "Patent Appeal: The Protection of Intellectual Property Rights in the American Automotive Sector, 1903-1911." Michigan Historical Review 49.1 (2023): 99-127.

Smith, Stefan Halikoswki. "Demystifying a change in taste: Spices, space, and social hierarchy in Europe, 1380–1750." The International history review 29.2 (2007): 237-257.

Sobel, Russell. "Regulation and Entrepreneurship: Theory, Impacts, and Implications." The Center for Growth and Opportunity (2023).

Spence, Janet T. "Achievement American style: The rewards and costs of individualism." American Psychologist 40.12 (1985): 1285.

Spenkuch, Jörg L. "The Protestant Ethic and work: Micro evidence from contemporary Germany." (2011).

Stiles, T. J. The first tycoon: The epic life of Cornelius Vanderbilt. Knopf, 2009.

Synnott, Marcia. The half-opened door: Discrimination and admissions at Harvard, Yale, and Princeton, 1900-1970. Routledge, 2017.

Teich, Mikulás, and Roy Porter, eds. The industrial revolution in national context: Europe and the USA. Cambridge University Press, 1996.

The Constitution for the United States, http://www.earlyamerica.com/earlyamerica/fre edom/constitution/text.html, (20.08.2011).

Thom McEvoy, Private Property Rights, A Look at Its History and Future, Fruit Notes, Volume 66, 2001, http://www.umas.edu/fruitadvisor/fruitnotes/p rivatepropertyrights.pdf., (20.08.2011).

Thomas H. Cox, Gibbons ve Ogden, Law, and Society in the Early Republic, Ohio University Press, 2009, s.10.

Thomas Jefferson, The Declaration of Independence, http://www.ushistory.org/Declaration/documen t/index.htm, (24.07.2012).

Thomas Terrell, The law and practice relating to letters patent for inventions, Forgotten Books, 2012, s.176-178.

Thomas, Roosevelt., Building on the Premise of Diversity, Amacom, 2005.

Uhler, Kevin A. The demise of patronage: Garfield, the midterm election, and the passage of the Pendleton Civil Service Act. Diss. The Florida State University, 2011.

Van Lange, Paul AM, and Jeff A. Joireman. "How we can promote behavior that serves all of us in the future." Social Issues and Policy Review 2.1 (2008): 127-157.

Vardi, Moshe Y. "Move fast and break things." Communications of the ACM 61.9 (2018): 7-7.

Vincent, Norah. Self-made man. London: Atlantic Books, 2006.

Vise, David A., and Mark Malseed. "The Google story: Inside the hottest business, media, and technology success of our time, paperback edition." New York: Delta Trade (2006).

Wallace, James, and Jim Erickson. Hard drive: Bill Gates and the making of the Microsoft empire. John Wiley & Sons, Inc., 1992.

Wallerstein, Immanuel. The modern world-system II: Mercantilism and the consolidation of the European world-economy, 1600–1750. Vol. 2. Univ of California Press, 2011.

Walterscheid, Edward C. "The early evolution of the United States patent law: Antecedents (Part 1)." J. Pat. & Trademark Off. Soc'y 76 (1994): 697.

Watanabe, Toshio, et al. "Benjamin Franklin: The Self-Made Man as an American Hero." The American Review 1977.11 (1977): 219-241.

Waterhouse, Benjamin C. The land of enterprise: A business history of the United States. Simon and Schuster, 2017.

Weber, Max. The Protestant work ethic and the spirit of capitalism. Allen and Unwin, 1976.

Wilf, Steven. "Intellectual Property." A Companion to American Legal History (2013): 441-459.

Wilson, Bee. Sandwich: A global history. Reaktion Books, 2010.

Wu, Lin, et al. "Short-term versus long-term benefits: Balanced sustainability framework and research propositions." Sustainable Production and Consumption 11 (2017): 18-30.

Xie, Rain. "Why China had to ban cryptocurrency but the US did not: a comparative analysis of regulations on crypto-markets between the US and China." Wash. U. Global Stud. L. Rev. 18 (2019): 457.

Xu, Teng Andrea, and Jiahua Xu. "A short survey on business models of decentralized finance (DeFi) protocols." arXiv preprint arXiv:2202.07742 (2022).

Yehoshua Arieli, Individualism and Nationalism in American Ideology, Penguin, 1966, s.345-346

Young, Jeffrey S., and William L. Simon. iCon Steve Jobs. John Wiley & Sons, 2006.

Young, Michael. The rise of the meritocracy. Routledge, 2017.

www.ingramcontent.com/pod-product-compliance
Lightning Source LLC
Chambersburg PA
CBHW030507210326
41597CB00013B/823